For all God's people

Ecumenical Prayer Cycle

World Council of Churches, Geneva

Cover design, maps and layout: Paul May

ISBN: 2-8254-0552-3

Printed in Switzerland

I kneel in prayer to the Father,
from whom every family in heaven and on earth takes its name,
that out of the treasures of his glory
he may grant you strength and power
through his Spirit in your inner being,
that through faith Christ may dwell in your hearts in love.
With deep roots and firm foundations,
may you be strong to grasp, with all God's people,
what is the breadth and length and height and depth
of the love of Christ,
and to know it, though it is beyond knowledge.
So may you attain to fullness of being,
the fullness of God himself.

Ephesians 3:14-19 (New English Bible)

Contents

Contents

Preface

". . . I am always praying for you in my intercessions" (Phil. 1:4). The Apostle Paul and the congregations which he had founded were one in a fellowship of mutual intercession. Cannot Christians today be united in the same fellowship?

Centuries of division have led to estrangements between the churches which are still far from overcome. But the walls of separation have begun to crumble. More and more we realize that, despite our differences, we form one family.

Let us therefore offer regular prayers of intercession for *all* who call upon the name of Christ. Intercession is an expression of fellowship in Christ and, at the same time, a means of strengthening it. In intercession we bring our fellow Christians before God and ask that his name be glorified in them (2 Thess. 1:12). Intercession need not be limited to those belonging to our own church. It can extend to all who seek to confess the love of God in Christ. Intercession anticipates the unity we are still seeking.

This book has been prepared as a tool to guide and deepen this kind of open intercession in both public worship and private prayers. The idea is very simple. For each week of the year the churches of a country or group of countries have been selected, with the suggestion that during that week intercessory prayers be offered for them in all the churches of the world. In this way all churches will visit in their prayers all other churches at least once a year. Four weeks of the year have been reserved for general themes of meditation and prayer.

For each week you will find four pages. The first gives a brief description of the group of churches and the country or countries in which they are situated, with some indication of their historical background and special characteristics. The information is necessarily far from exhaustive and should be regarded as no more than an introductory sketch. The next page provides a map with a list of the churches located in the region. Page three is headed "For Prayer". There you will find biddings for thanksgiving and intercession, followed by a prayer derived from the region or in common use there. The fourth page is especially important; it is left blank and is reserved for your own notes and comments. You may want to list there the people you have met or heard about, especially people in difficult situations and suffering for their faith. You may use the page to remind yourself of the problems, tensions and conflicts which certain churches are facing. This page is meant as an invitation to translate your personal knowledge of other churches and Christians into regular intercessory prayers.[1]

Jesus' Prayer

Intercession has its roots in the prayer of Jesus Christ. Before ever we began to pray, he prayed for us—for his disciples and for *all* who, through the disciples, would believe in him. Intercession is participation in his intercession for his people: "Father, I pray for them". It is helpful to recall the occasion of this prayer. It was the prayer of Jesus at the very moment when his work was accomplished and he offered his life and blood for the salvation of all. His intercession announces his self-giving. His life and death can be understood and described as one great decisive act of intercession. "Father, forgive them, they do not know what they are doing" was his prayer shortly before dying on the cross. God heard his prayer. He raised him from the dead and set him

---

1. For more detailed suggestions about possible uses of the book, see pp. 223-229.

at his own right hand. His intercession has not come to an end with his death. As in his life on earth, the risen Christ continues to "intercede for us" (Rom. 8:34).

Prayer, intercessory prayer especially, is not a matter of course. We do not have a natural "religious capacity" for prayer. We need the Holy Spirit to give us access to God and to teach us how to pray. Prayer means making room for the Spirit that he may pray in us. "We do not know how we ought to pray", says Paul, "but through our inarticulate groans the Spirit himself is pleading for us and God who searches our inmost being knows what the Spirit means because he pleads for God's people in God's own way" (Rom. 8:26-28). Prayer in Christ will always include intercession, too. As we pray in him, we shall be drawn into his love for all. We shall not be concerned exclusively with ourselves. Our attention will be turned to others.

Our horizons are limited, of course. To include every single fellow Christian in our prayers is beyond our human capacity. There is even wisdom in concentrating on specific persons and problems. At the same time, however, Christ wants us to keep in mind the life and witness of the whole Church. His intercession reaches out to all God's people. Participation in his prayer puts in our hearts, therefore, a concern for the whole Church scattered over all the earth. The prayer cycle offered in this book is meant simply as an instrument to widen our horizons and to deepen our sense of participation in the life and witness of the whole Church.

Baptized in the Name of Christ

Calling upon the name of Christ means more than giving allegiance to a cause. It means being drawn into his death and resurrection. For most of us this identification with Christ takes place at the moment of baptism. For what is baptism but being "buried with Christ in order that, as Christ was raised from the dead in the splendour of the Father, so also we might set our feet upon the new path of life" (Rom. 6:4).

New birth, new life, new fellowship! Baptism carries all these meanings. It is a powerful bond holding us together even though we still live in separate churches. Bearing the sign of baptism, we are, in a certain sense, already one.

Baptism reminds us of the nature of fellowship and unity in Christ. Unity is both given and constantly to be established. Christ *has* come. He *has* died. He *has* been raised to new life. In the power of the Spirit we *have* access to God's grace and have been given everything necessary for life in a new fellowship. Potentially, the causes of hostility have already been overcome. At the same time, the quality of the fellowship depends on our obedience and commitment. The gift can be and is constantly being betrayed. We are all called to participate in the construction of fellowship and unity in Christ.

Intercession is part of this task. We need constantly to pray that the gift of unity may become manifest in its original purity; that the enmities and obstacles which keep us apart may be removed; that we may be enabled to recognize in each other's witness the same apostolic faith; that we who have been baptized in the name of Christ may also be enabled to celebrate the eucharist together. We need to pray that nothing may have power to obscure the fellowship we have already been granted; that we may be given the grace to confess Christ; that we may be strengthened to face principalities and powers and to stand with those who suffer injustice; that communication between our churches may not fail and, where it has failed, may be renewed.

8

Thanksgiving and Witness

The starting point of intercession is thanksgiving. We turn to God to praise him for the blessings he has bestowed and continues to bestow on every church and on every community of Christians. Almost all of Paul's letters begin with thanksgiving and praise. There are good reasons for putting thanksgiving first. If we at once concentrate on petitions, our attention may focus too exclusively on aspects which may be thought missing in the life of other churches. Intercession can be distorted into a subtle paternalism. We think of others and ask that *they* may be given strength to grow.

To set our intercessions in the right perspective, the starting point for our prayers should be God's action in his Church. Let us thank him for the manifold gifts he grants; for the witness borne to Christ in innumerable places; for the insights and encouragement which we receive from other churches. Let us pray that *we* may be open for the enrichment which other churches may share with us.

Then, in this spirit of thanksgiving, we can go on to ask also for new blessings, both for ourselves and for others; that we may all grow in understanding of the Gospel; that new doors may be opened for the proclamation of the same; that good words may be found for speaking the truth; that strength may be given to stand firm under suffering and persecution. Ultimately, intercessory prayers have only a single theme, the unity and the witness of the Christian family.

Intercession as Solidarity

But is intercessory prayer enough? Does it not need to be followed, will it not necessarily be followed, by more concrete acts of solidarity? Indeed it does and it will. There is no tension or contradiction between intercession and solidarity. Intercession calls for acts of solidarity and is itself an act of solidarity. Intercession directs our hearts to others. It seeks before God an understanding of their real needs and how these needs could perhaps be met. Intercession is the first step towards a fuller manifestation of mutual love.

The prayer cycle is an important instrument in this respect. It offers the churches an opportunity for evaluating their relationship with other churches. When praying for the churches of a certain region, they will need to ask such questions as this: What does the witness of these churches mean for the life of our own churches? What can *we* do to strengthen their witness? What have we done in their support? What should we have done but failed to do?

But the capacity of human solidarity is also limited. To deal effectively with problems, injustice and suffering is not something which depends solely on the sincerity of our efforts. Situations often cannot be changed and must be accepted. The recognition of our narrow limits is for many a source of despair. Is there really no way of winning the struggle against injustice? Intercession can save us from such despair. God does not expect us to perfect the world. He himself leads it to its fulfilment. We small human beings can only point to his action and perhaps establish provisional signs of it by loving action. Intercession makes us aware both of our calling and of our human limitations.

About this Book

This book is a direct response to the clear call of the Fifth Assembly of the World Council of Churches in Nairobi to deepen the spiritual bonds among the churches. The report on the unity of the Church, for example, recommended "that all churches should encourage and assist their members in regular and informed intercession for the other churches".

The prayer cycle is one attempt to put this recommendation into practice. It has been the custom now for many years in the Ecumenical Centre in Geneva to offer intercessory prayers for the churches of the world every morning. Why not make this cycle available to all the churches? Why not include in the list, not just member churches, but all churches confessing Jesus Christ as God and Saviour?

The suggestion met with a swift and favourable response. The World Alliance of Reformed Churches and the Lutheran World Federation offered their full collaboration from the very beginning. The Methodist and Baptist world bodies expressed their interest and have provided valuable help. The annual meeting in preparation for the Week of Prayer for Christian Unity, sponsored by the Vatican Secretariat for Promoting Christian Unity and the Faith and Order Commission, provided the opportunity for widening the scope of the project and agreement was soon reached on the inclusion of the Roman Catholic Church in the lists for each week. In a certain sense, the prayer cycle can be seen as the prolongation of the Week of Prayer for Christian Unity throughout the whole year.

Responsibility for the project was borne primarily by the WCC Faith and Order Commission and the sub-unit on Renewal and Congregational Life. A small editorial committee was formed to prepare the material for publication. So many colleagues and friends in the Ecumenical Centre and elsewhere have been involved in the gestation of this ecumenical prayer cycle that only a "general thanksgiving" for all the help so readily given is possible.

It will be realized that to present in summary form a guide to the whole *oikumene* represents a difficult if not impossible undertaking. Repeated attempts have been made to check and counter-check the drafts at successive stages but inevitably mistakes and serious omissions will still be found. The indulgence and forgiveness of those affected by these errors is asked in advance. No doubt, too, the presentation can still be improved. Indeed, the most appropriate way of presenting the material will probably only become apparent as the cycle is used in practice.

The present text, therefore, is to be regarded as provisional. It is made available in the expectation that, at the appropriate time, a new version will be prepared on the basis of the experience gained in its practical use in the churches and in the light of the corrections and suggestions received.

Do everything in common:
Unite in one prayer, one petition,
one mind, one hope,
in love and faultless joy.
All this is Jesus Christ,
and there is nothing better than he.
So make haste, all of you,
to come together as to one temple of God,
around one altar,
around the one Jesus Christ,
who came forth from the one Father,
while still remaining one with him,
and has returned to unity with him.

St. Ignatius of Antioch (c. 115 AD)
Letter to the Magnesians

11

Index of countries according to weeks

Week 1

Israel, Egypt, Jordan, Lebanon and Syria

Nowhere in the world are the divisions of Christianity more manifest than in *Jerusalem.* The Greek Orthodox Patriarchate of Jerusalem is the oldest church, having been elevated to a Patriarchate in 451. Today it has a membership of about 80,000 in Jordan and Israel. The Armenian Patriarchate of Jerusalem cares for the spiritual needs of Armenian communities in Israel and Jordan.

The Roman Catholic Church has a Greek Catholic Bishop in Haifa and a Latin Patriarch in Jerusalem responsible for the faithful scattered over Israel, Jordan and Cyprus. The 19th century saw the beginning of missionary activity by Protestants. It resulted in the formation of churches that are numerically small but in several cases ecumenically active.

In *Egypt*, the Church of Alexandria dates back to the Apostles. Early church fathers like Clement, Origen, Athanasius and Cyril worked there, and there too developed the first forms of monastic life.

Following a rift in the 5th century, this Church formed two branches: the Coptic Orthodox with a membership of approximately 6 million mainly in Egypt and Sudan, and the Greek Orthodox Patriarchate of Alexandria which ministers to some 400,000 faithful in Cairo, Alexandria and elsewhere in Africa. There are also a number of Roman Catholics belonging to several rites, each closely linked with a particular nation of origin. A small Presbyterian Church came into being in Egypt during the last century.

To the north of Jerusalem is the Greek Orthodox Patriarchate of Antioch, one of the most ancient churches. With its See now in Damascus, it serves a membership of about 1 million spread over Syria and Lebanon with strong diaspora communities in North and South America and Australia.

In *Lebanon* the Maronites are the largest Christian church. Their origin dates from the 7th century when, persecuted by other Christians, they sought refuge in the Lebanese moutains. This is an autonomous church in communion with the Holy See.

The Armenian Catholicossate of Cilicia was founded in the 11th century after the destruction of the Armenian capital. At that time many Armenians settled in Cilicia where they established a kingdom known as Little Armenia and reorganized their ecclesiastical and national life. After the massacres at the beginning of this century, the catholicossate was transferred to Antelias in Lebanon whence the Catholicos now serves faithful scattered in diaspora throughout many countries.

Evangelical churches of Presbyterian provenance, as well as the Union of Armenian Evangelical Churches in the Near East, are working in Syria and Lebanon.

With all the peoples of this region, Christians share in the troubles and sufferings caused by wars, social and political unrest. The churches' tasks are manifold, but high among their priorities is the work for peace, reconciliation and mutual understanding.

Armenian Catholicossate in Ciclicia
Armenian Patriarchate of Jerusalem
Association of Baptist Churches in Israel
Coptic Orthodox Church
Episcopal Church in Jerusalem and the Middle East
Evangelical Church – Synod of the Nile
Evangelical Synod of Syria and Lebanon
Free Methodist Church – Egypt
Greek Orthodox Patriarchate of Alexandria
Greek Orthodox Patriarchate of Antioch
Greek Orthodox Patriarchate of Jerusalem
Lebanon Baptist Convention
Lutheran Church (Haknesi Haluteranit)
Roman Catholic Church in the Arab Regions
Union of Armenian Evangelical Churches in the Near East

Include in your prayers all ecumenical councils and working groups at local or national level

Remember also all Christian movements and communities which seek to proclaim and serve Jesus Christ

For Prayer and Intercession

Give thanks . . .   for Jerusalem and all it has given to humanity;
for the Jewish people from whom Jesus Christ came, their prophets and apostles;
for the great teachers and leaders of the Church in Alexandria and Antioch;
for the monastic life which originated in Egypt and its contribution to the life of the churches throughout the ages.

Pray . . .   for peace in the Middle East; for mutual trust and courageous acts of reconciliation;
for unity among the Christian churches and genuine dialogue with people who confess other faiths;
for fruitful and committed work for all who are poor, displaced or uprooted.

Prayer . . .   O Master, Lord, God Almighty, Father of our Lord, our God, our Saviour Jesus Christ, we thank thee upon every condition, for any condition and in whatever condition. For thou hast covered us, supported us, preserved us, accepted us unto thee, had compassion on us, sustained us and brought us unto this hour. Wherefore we pray and entreat thy goodness, O lover-of-mankind, grant us to complete this holy day and all the days of our life in all peace with thy fear.

Thanksgiving Prayer from the Coptic Liturgy

For your own notes

North Africa and the Sahel

From the days of Simon of Cyrene, a church was established in North Africa. The homes of such major Christian figures as Cyprian and Augustine, however, were overrun by nomadic invaders long before the new order brought by Islam. Islam itself failed deeply to penetrate some of the Berber tribes such as the Kabyles; among these tribes and among the European immigrants to North Africa small Roman Catholic and Protestant churches were established from the 19th century.

Partly because of their solidarity with the new nationalist movements these small churches have survived, albeit with reduced numbers. Ecumenical initiatives in recent years include the formation, in 1978, of the Council of Christian Churches of Morocco, which embraces the Roman Catholic Church, the Greek and Russian Orthodox churches, the Anglican Church and the Evangelical Church of Morocco.

Many church buildings have been donated for community welfare and recreation purposes; some large church buildings, including one or two which originally had been built on the site of mosques, have been sold or donated to governments and converted into mosques. The few resident or visiting Christians today work alongside Muslims, including many more secular-minded men and women. Christian institutions and projects are often in close liaison with governments which welcome such cooperation; for example, Algeria has Christians working on government projects. In the Sahel drought zone of Senegal, Mali, Upper Volta, etc., Christians and Muslims work together in environmental teams in literally hundreds of local situations. Churches are engaged in respectful study of their Muslim neighbours and Muslims are taking the initiative to enlist the collaboration of Christians. Christian evangelical work is mostly patient and discreet and some use is made of radio programmes from abroad.

A major point of contact with North African Muslims is now provided by their emigration, sometimes temporary, to France (where they are three times as numerous as the Protestants) and other European countries. The churches' solidarity — or lack of solidarity — with these North Africans can have far-reaching effects.

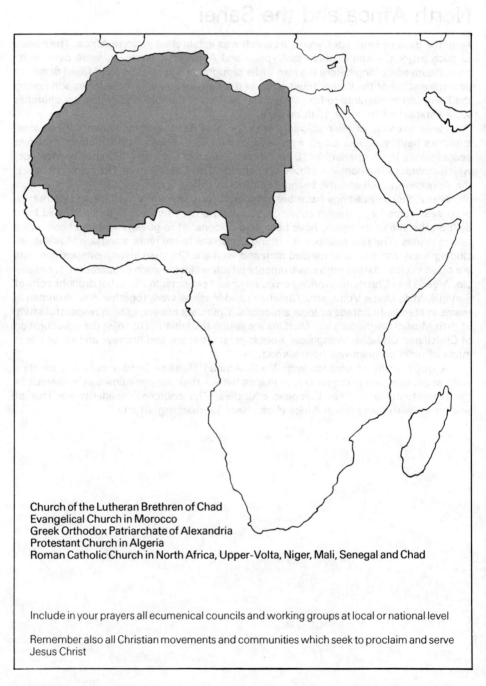

Church of the Lutheran Brethren of Chad
Evangelical Church in Morocco
Greek Orthodox Patriarchate of Alexandria
Protestant Church in Algeria
Roman Catholic Church in North Africa, Upper-Volta, Niger, Mali, Senegal and Chad

Include in your prayers all ecumenical councils and working groups at local or national level

Remember also all Christian movements and communities which seek to proclaim and serve Jesus Christ

For Prayer and Intercession

Give thanks . . .   for the church fathers who lived in North Africa yet whose insights have enriched the whole world.

Pray . . .   for those few who witness for Christ in North Africa and the Sahel today:
for their bonds of fellowship within their small churches and their sense of being upheld by Christians elsewhere;
for their courageous and creative cooperation in nation-building together with their Muslim neighbours;
for their discernment of neglected or unfinished tasks especially among the sick, the hungry, the very poor.

Pray . . .   for the predominantly Muslim neighbours of these churches:
for their devotion to God and reverence for Jesus;
for their wrestlings both with poverty and with new riches;
for their relationships with Christians whom they hear and meet, or with whom they work.

Prayer . . .   O thou, from whom to be turned is to fall,
to whom to be turned is to rise,
and in whom to stand is to abide for ever;
Grant us in all our duties thy help,
in all our perplexities thy guidance,
in all our dangers thy protection,
and in all our sorrows thy peace;
through Jesus Christ our Lord.

St. Augustine of Hippo

For your own notes

Week 3

Our Community

Praying week by week for churches in every part of the world, your vision of Christ's Church is enlarged. This week, however, shorten your vision and take a new look at your own neighbourhood. Think of God's people who live next door or down the road.

Our neighbourhoods are very different. Yours may be a small village or a huge apartment building. The people around you are very different—in colour, language, religion or whatever—from those who surround others using this prayer guide. Of course, we have much in common, too. The whole world has been touched by vast exchanges of peoples and ideas in recent years. Few neighbourhoods exhibit the uniformity of previous eras. Some of the people around you may be new, with different languages and customs. Perhaps you are the new and different people in the community. Even more easily than people, ideas have flowed around the world, bringing new insights and new divisions.

Our encounters with people who are different from ourselves and who think different thoughts may be enriching experiences which help us all toward the truth of God. They may, on the other hand, push us toward isolation and alienation. Will the differentness of some people in your community be a source of enrichment or a source of conflict? The answer may depend on the Church's ministry of reconciliation.

Through our prayers we reach out to those who live around us. We may be able to call their names, or we may have caught only a glimpse of them in passing. Our prayers affirm their worth to us because they, too, are children of God and therefore of infinite worth to him. Prayer, in fact, may be the first step towards friendship and trust.

Yet . . . in many places there are churches of different denominations on every street corner, or misunderstandings which have given rise to factions within our churches. As you pray for healing in the community, pray too for reconciliation within the Church and for all work which churches do together in your community.

You may also find around you people of different religious faiths and some who confess no religious faith at all—perhaps people who have abandoned the Church to seek religious truth in other ways, or young people disillusioned by the imperfections of the familiar Christian institution and seek new spiritual life in new kinds of communities. Pray for them, too, and for opportunities to grow with these people in mutual appreciation and understanding.

And give special thanks for those who are closest to you: your family and close friends, whose support and love sustain you day by day. They are God's precious gifts.

For Prayer and Intercession

Give thanks . . .   for the place where we live;

for those with whom we share common bonds of heritage, religious convictions, and family ties;

for our church, for other churches, and for the special gifts each gives to our community;

for all the variety of the human race;

for the enrichment of life in community with people of other heritages, colours, and religious faiths.

Pray . . .   that the churches of our neighbourhood may be renewed in the faith and mission of Jesus Christ whom we confess together as Lord;

that the churches will give themselves to ministries of reconciliation in the Body of Christ, so that the Church may again one day exhibit the unity which is the will and the gift of God;

that the churches may join together in ministries of reconciliation within the community, speaking and acting against all sources of injustice and prejudice;

that the people who live together in our place may discover in their common humanity sufficient reason to join in relationships of support and trust;

Let us add those petitions of thanksgiving and intercession appropriate for our own community, village, or neighbourhood.

Prayer . . .   O God, our Father, we thank thee for our home and family; for love and forbearance, for friends and foes,

for laughter enjoyed and sorrow shared, for the daily bread of thy bounty in good times and bad. Help us to be mindful of thy gifts and glad to show forth thy praise; through Jesus Christ our Lord.

R. N. Rodenmayer

For your own notes

Week 4

Ethiopia, Sudan, Somalia and Djibouti

Ethiopia's 26 million people have been ruled since 1974 by a Provisional Military Council which took power from Emperor Haile Selassie and declared "Ethiopian socialism". The sweeping change included a radical land reform, but the political situation remains extremely fluid. There is fighting within and on the frontiers. Eritrea, under Italian rule from the end of the 19th century until 1941, then under British administration, was united with Ethiopia in 1962, but struggles for independence have continued.

Since the military takeover, all nationalities, languages and religions have been declared equal. Thus Orthodoxy which claims about 10 million adherents has lost its status as state religion and the Sufi Muslims (also about 10 million, organized around many holy places) have for the first time achieved equal rights. Orthodoxy came to Ethiopia in the 4th century. The Ethiopian Orthodox Church, a founding member of the WCC, is one of the Oriental Orthodox churches which did not accept the christological dogma of the Council of Chalcedon (451). Independent of the Coptic Orthodox Church of Egypt since 1959, the Ethiopian Church now elects its own Patriarchs.

Apart from Orthodox, there is the Roman Catholic Church with about 150,000 members, some two-thirds belonging to the Coptic rite. Protestants number about 600,000. They stem from the work of a variety of mission societies from Scandinavia, Germany and the United States. Congregations established by the former Sudan Interior Mission, now the African Inland Church, form the largest Protestant group, numbering about 300,000. The Evangelical Church Mekane Yesus (285,000 members) originated from Lutheran mission efforts. There are several smaller Lutheran, Mennonite and Pentecostal groups.

"Ethiopian socialism" confronts all the churches with immense questions. Large land holdings, which were an important source of income for the Orthodox Church especially, have been nationalized. The hundreds of missionaries may not be able to stay in the country. The large subsidies from churches overseas may not be allowed to continue.

Bordering Ethiopia to the west is the *Sudan* where Christianity was widespread before Muslim control was established around 1500. The Democratic Republic of Sudan has an Islamic constitution but grants religious liberty to all faiths. The Christian churches together have about half a million members (i.e. 10% of the total population). Apart from the 300,000 Roman Catholics, the Coptic Orthodox Church is found in the northern part of the country whereas Protestant churches live mostly in the south.

In 1965 the Sudan Christian Council was founded. It links Roman Catholic, Coptic, Anglican, Presbyterian and African Inland churches, and has played a key role in efforts towards national reconstruction since the peace settlement in 1972.

To the East are *Somalia* and *Djibouti* which border on the gulf of Aden. Islam is the faith of the people here, almost without exception.

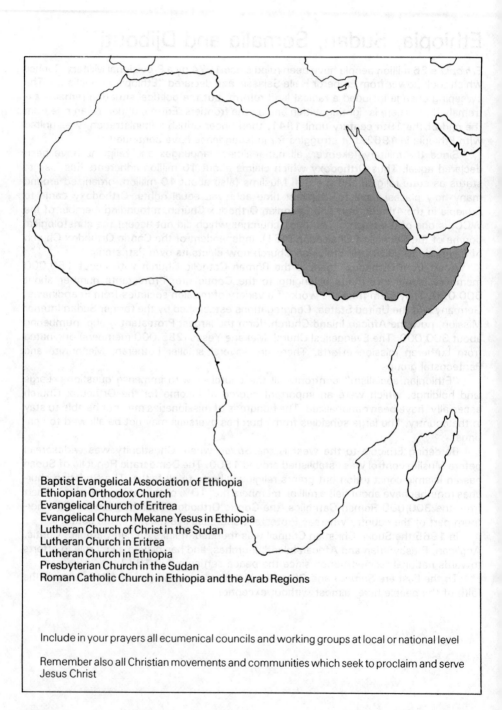

Baptist Evangelical Association of Ethiopia
Ethiopian Orthodox Church
Evangelical Church of Eritrea
Evangelical Church Mekane Yesus in Ethiopia
Lutheran Church of Christ in the Sudan
Lutheran Church in Eritrea
Lutheran Church in Ethiopia
Presbyterian Church in the Sudan
Roman Catholic Church in Ethiopia and the Arab Regions

Include in your prayers all ecumenical councils and working groups at local or national level

Remember also all Christian movements and communities which seek to proclaim and serve
Jesus Christ

For Prayer and Intercession

Give thanks . . .   for all who, through the ages, have proclaimed and served the Lord in honesty and love;
for all genuine efforts to preach the Good News to the poor and to bridge tensions, wars and conflicts in the spirit of peace.

Pray . . .   for peace in the region and harmony between its peoples;
that the churches may face revolutionary political and social changes with courage, humility and imagination;
for the building of strong links between the churches, and between Christians and their neighbours of other faiths.

Prayer . . .   Lord our God and our Saviour and lover of mankind, thou art he who didst send thy holy disciples and ministers, and thy pure apostles unto all the ends of the world to preach and teach the Gospel of thy kingdom, and to heal all the diseases and all the sicknesses which are among thy people, and to proclaim the mystery hidden from before the beginning of the world.
Now also, our Lord and our God, send upon us thy light and thy righteousness, and enlighten the eyes of our hearts and of our understanding; make us worthy to persevere in hearing the word of thy holy Gospel, and not only to hear but to do according to what we hear, so that it may bear good fruit in us, remaining not one only but increasing thirty, sixty, and an hundredfold; and forgive us our sins, us thy people, so that we may be worthy of the kingdom of heaven.

Liturgy of the Ethiopian Orthodox Church

For your own notes

Week 5

Cape Verde, The Gambia, Guinea Bissau, Guinea, Liberia, Senegal and Sierra Leone

Christianity reached these West African countries in the mid-15th century, when Roman Catholic priests from Portugal ministered to small communities of Portuguese slave traders with their African or Mulatto families, scattered along the Gambia and neighbouring rivers. For the most part the African population lived in small, semi-independent states and adhered to indigenous religions. Only a few Muslim traders/teachers had wandered through the region from Mauritania in the north.

With the evangelical awakening, the activities of missionary societies in West Africa found an immediate response from freed black slaves living in Freetown, Bathurst, Conakry, Monrovia, largely because of the abolition of the Atlantic slave trade (1807) and slavery (1833). They had been exposed to Christianity during slavery in Canada, USA and the West Indies; and now returned to Africa to become, in some cases, themselves missionaries. By the mid-19th century, Protestant Missions, joined by the Roman Catholic Holy Ghost Fathers and the Sisters of St. Joseph of Cluny, had established churches and educational institutions, and were engaged in agricultural and industrial projects. Sierra Leone gave the lead.

Meanwhile, Islam was entering the Sene-Gambia region, through Muslim traders. During the second half of the 19th century, the whole West African hinterland had come under direct Muslim control. Islamic power, however, was crushed by aggressive European powers by the end of the century. Only the American-sponsored state of Liberia retained its political independence. For the rest, it was not till the 1960's and 1970's that they regained independence from their European masters.

Since the 1950's most Protestant churches have developed indigenous leadership. More and more churches have forged links with each other, even across political frontiers. This is of vital importance in an area where Christians form such a small minority of the total population—from a mere 5% in The Gambia to 15% in Liberia.

The churches' greatest concern is for their work and witness in predominantly Islamic societies, where Muslim influence is expanding through medical and educational work which used to be almost the preserve of Christian missions. Though state constitutions safeguard freedom of worship and foreign missions are still permitted to operate, the Christian minority remains apprehensive. All these churches are trying to become self-supporting and to end their dependence on churches in Europe and North America. The difficulties involved, however, are considerable.

African Methodist Episcopal Church
African Methodist Episcopal Zion Church
Church of the Province of West Africa
Liberia Baptist Missionary and Educational Convention, Inc.
Lutheran Church in Liberia
Methodist Church – The Gambia and Sierra Leone
Presbytery of Liberia in West Africa
Protestant Church of Senegal
Roman Catholic Church in the Republic of Guinea Bissau, in Senegal and Mauritania,
   in Liberia, Sierra Leone and Gambia
United Methodist Church – Liberia and Sierra Leone

Include in your prayers all ecumenical councils and working groups at local or national level

Remember also all Christian movements and communities which seek to proclaim and serve
Jesus Christ

For Prayer and Intercession

Give thanks . . .

for those who, in slavery, heeded Christ's promise of freedom and joy, and themselves became his witnesses;
for those Christians and Muslims who are trying to build bridges of understanding between the two religious communities.

Pray . . .

for churches seeking a clearer vision of their identity and role in post-colonial West Africa;
for national Christian councils and all other initiatives aimed at healing divisions among the churches;
for an end to excessive dependence, and the growth of true mutuality between these churches and their opposite numbers abroad.

Prayer . . .

Come, Lord, and cover me with the night. Spread your grace over us as you assured us you would do.
Your promises are more than all the stars in the sky;
Your mercy is deeper than the night.
Lord, it will be cold.
The night comes with its breath of death.
Night comes, the end comes,
but Jesus Christ comes also.
Lord, we wait for him day and night. Amen.

A prayer from West Africa

For your own notes

Ivory Coast, Ghana, Togo and Benin

A common history of colonialism has left its mark on these nations, which are divided by arbitrary boundaries established by the colonizers without regard to ethnic territories. European governments exploited the land, and the people were unable to control their own lives. Beginning in the 16th century and reaching its peak in the late 17th and early 18th centuries, slave traders invaded the land and sold the people.

Ghana, the most populous of the nations with more than 9 million inhabitants, gained freedom from Britain in 1957. Ivory Coast, Togo and Benin achieved independence from France in 1960. All except Ivory Coast have experienced coup d'états and are currently under military rule.

Christian missionaries arrived with the colonizers and traders between the 15th and 19th centuries. From 40% to 60% of the people continue to follow traditional animist beliefs. Christians range from 12% in Ivory Coast to nearly 52% in Ghana. In Benin and Ivory Coast, Roman Catholics outnumber the Protestants. Muslims range from 3% in Benin to 23% in Ivory Coast.

Christian missionary societies pioneered in education, opening a number of schools and colleges. For some years several churches in Ghana have been engaged in union negotiations, now at a rather crucial stage. Meanwhile, cooperation between the various Protestant churches and, in some instances, with the Roman Catholic Church has been growing. Independent churches have increased in recent years, attracting large numbers and posing a challenge to the older, established churches.

There is a growing awareness of the necessity to free the churches from liturgical forms which are reminders of the colonial period and which neglect the riches of the African heritage. The recovery of forms of worship and proclamation relevant within an African context will enable the churches to be more effective in their evangelism and in their witness.

African Methodist Episcopal Church
African Methodist Episcopal Zion Church
Christian Methodist Episcopal Church
Church of the Province of West Africa
Evangelical Church of Togo
Evangelical Lutheran Church of Ghana
Evangelical Presbyterian Church, Ghana
Ghana Baptist Convention
Methodist Church, Ghana
Presbyterian Church of Ghana
Protestant Methodist Church in Benin-Togo
Roman Catholic Church of Benin, Ghana, Ivory Coast and Togo
Salvation Army
Togo Baptist Association

Include in your prayers all ecumenical councils and working groups at local or national level

Remember also all Christian movements and communities which seek to proclaim and serve Jesus Christ

For Prayer and Intercession

Give thanks . . . for the rapid growth of the Christian faith in the countries of Ivory Coast, Ghana, Togo and Benin;
for the enduring and steadfast search for unity among the churches;
for their zeal to proclaim the Good News of Christ to all people.

Pray . . . for the overcoming of imported divisions between the churches, for union negotiations now in a crucial stage and for the achievement of full unity;
for the reconciliation of tensions between ethnic groups;
for success in the struggle against starvation, injustice and dependency.

Prayer . . . O Lord, our heavenly Father,
You hear us praying here in Takoradi.
You hear our brothers and sisters
praying in Africa, in Asia, in Australia,
in America and in Europe.
We are all one in prayer.
We praise and honour you,
and we beg you
that we may rightly carry out your commission:
to witness and to love,
in our church and throughout the whole world.
Accept our prayers graciously,
even when they are somewhat strange.
We praise you and pray to you
through Jesus Christ, our Lord.

A prayer from Ghana

For your own notes

Nigeria

Nigeria is a huge and complex country with a population of over 70 million and many ethnic communities, languages and cultures. There are three major religions: Christianity, Islam, and the traditional African religions. Christians number roughly 20 million, divided more or less equally between Roman Catholics and Protestants.

First contacts between Western Europe and West Africa date from the end of the 15th century. Until the 19th century, the Europeans were primarily interested in the export of Africans as slaves to the Americas. With the abolition of slavery in the early years of the 19th century, Europeans began to explore Africa and energetic missionary activity followed.

Methodists began work prior to 1840 in response to the return of ex-slaves, Anglicans in 1844, Presbyterians from Scotland in 1846, Baptists from the USA in 1850, Roman Catholics in 1860 and Lutherans in 1912. From their work grew many of the 25 denominations now found in Nigeria. Independent churches, some originating inside Nigeria, have added to the number of denominations.

Ecumenical cooperation among Protestant churches began early this century, especially in the eastern area, with Anglican, Methodist, and Presbyterian churches agreeing first on comity, then on the creation of a common theological college and joint efforts in teacher training and hospital work. There has been a movement toward church unity, but the inauguration of the union scheduled for December 1965 had to be postponed. A number of the main Protestant churches pursue common reflection and action in the Christian Council of Nigeria, through which they sometimes address themselves to issues of national importance. Joint efforts are also accomplished through the Bible Society of Nigeria.

The churches face many challenges. The number of unemployed school-leavers grows yearly. The soaring cost of living is widening the gap between rich and poor, making it difficult for the churches to afford the educated personnel they need. Forms and structures of church life need to be developed to replace the inherited structures which hamper the main-line churches. The replacement of missionaries by Nigerians in recent years is only one step in that direction.

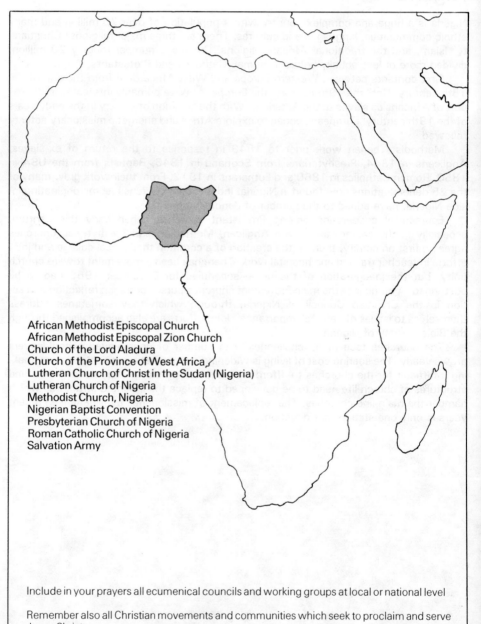

African Methodist Episcopal Church
African Methodist Episcopal Zion Church
Church of the Lord Aladura
Church of the Province of West Africa
Lutheran Church of Christ in the Sudan (Nigeria)
Lutheran Church of Nigeria
Methodist Church, Nigeria
Nigerian Baptist Convention
Presbyterian Church of Nigeria
Roman Catholic Church of Nigeria
Salvation Army

Include in your prayers all ecumenical councils and working groups at local or national level

Remember also all Christian movements and communities which seek to proclaim and serve Jesus Christ

For Prayer and Intercession

Give thanks . . .

for the sowing of the seed of the Gospel in Nigeria, and the establishment and growth of the Church;

for the material and spiritual services which the churches are still giving to Nigeria through their proclamation, Bible translation, education, medicine and healing, and other ministries;

for the autonomy of the churches, the development of indigenous leadership, efforts at self-help and self-reliance.

Pray . . .

that the churches may be renewed in worship, mission and service, that the Word may spread and grow so that more and more may believe and be saved;

that the churches may catch a new vision of their fellowship in Christ, to free them from arrogant use of their autonomy and open the way towards a united church in Nigeria;

that the churches may be endowed by the Spirit with holiness and boldness, to promote freedom, justice, love and reconciliation and a healthy community.

Prayer . . .

Oh God of Abraham, God of Isaac and God of Jacob, the beginning and the end: without you we can do nothing. The great river is not big enough for you to wash your hands in. You have the yam and you have the knife; we cannot eat unless you cut us a piece. We are like ants in your sight. We are like little children who only wash their stomach when they bath, leaving their back dry.

Chinua Achebe

For your own notes

Cameroon and Central African Empire

It was in the 1840's that two Baptist ministers, a Jamaican and a Briton, first brought the Gospel to *Cameroon*. The Union of Baptist Churches in Cameroon originates from this early evangelism. After the German takeover of the Cameroons, the London Baptist Mission was replaced by the Basel Mission in 1886. This in turn gave birth to the Presbyterian Church in Cameroon. In 1886 American Presbyterians began work in the South of Cameroon. From this mission grew the Eglise Presbytérienne Camerounaise and in 1935, following a language conflict, the Eglise Protestante Africaine. German Catholic missionaries arrived in 1890. The capital and the central regions became almost totally Catholic, and subsequently this church spread throughout the country. Its hierarchy was established in 1955.

The Basel Mission, expelled by the French, was replaced by the American Presbyterian Mission and the Paris Mission. From the latter grew the Evangelical Church of Cameroon.

Northern Cameroon was evangelized by Roman Catholic missions from 1914 and then by Protestants (American Lutherans) from 1920. These churches remain minorities and have occasionally been subjected to persecution. From these missions grew the Evangelical Lutheran Church of Cameroon and the Church of Lutheran Brethren.

Protestant missions joined to form the Evangelical Federation of Cameroon and French Equatorial Africa. With the independence of the countries involved, this federation split up. The churches of Cameroon created the Federation of Evangelical Churches and Missions in Cameroon (FEMEC) which brings together 13 churches and missions including some which are not members of the World Council of Churches. This Federation coordinates activities in such fields as education, health, development, information and evangelism.

The Central African Republic became independent in 1960 and proclaimed itself the *Central African Empire* in 1976. The Roman Catholic Church set up its first mission in 1894 near Bangui, the capital; but the missionary activities really only spread from 1919. In 1920 Protestant missions of American Baptist and Brethren origin arrived. In 1960 there were 150,000 Catholics and 111,000 Protestants in the Central African Republic, of a total population of 1,200,000.

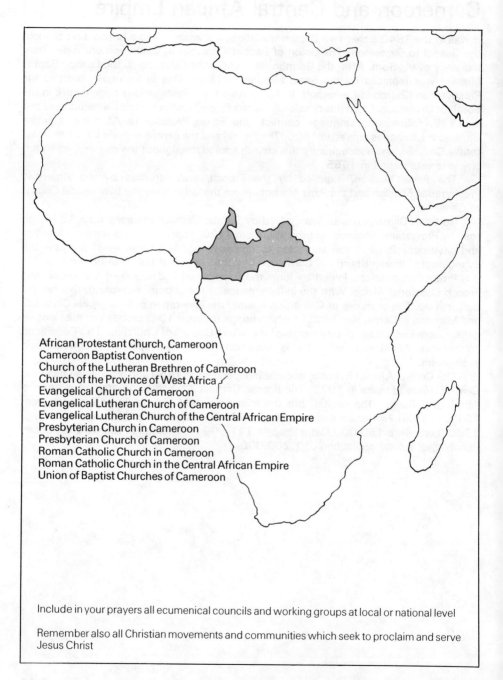

African Protestant Church, Cameroon
Cameroon Baptist Convention
Church of the Lutheran Brethren of Cameroon
Church of the Province of West Africa
Evangelical Church of Cameroon
Evangelical Lutheran Church of Cameroon
Evangelical Lutheran Church of the Central African Empire
Presbyterian Church in Cameroon
Presbyterian Church of Cameroon
Roman Catholic Church in Cameroon
Roman Catholic Church in the Central African Empire
Union of Baptist Churches of Cameroon

Include in your prayers all ecumenical councils and working groups at local or national level

Remember also all Christian movements and communities which seek to proclaim and serve Jesus Christ

For Prayer and Intercession

Give thanks . . .   for the vision and fidelity of those who first carried the Gospel to this area;
for the evangelical witness of these churches today;
for efforts towards reconciling divided Christians, especially the work of the Federation of Evangelical Churches and Missions in Cameroon.

Pray . . .   that divisions among Christians resulting from the accidents of history—language differences, colonial policies, decisions by overseas mission boards—may be overcome;
that the churches may find their rightful place in the struggle for economic development, social justice and human dignity;
that the leaders of these churches may be faithful servants of Christ's people.

Prayer . . .   I am happy because you have accepted me, dear Lord.
Sometimes I do not know what to do with all my happiness.
I swim in your grace like a whale in the ocean.
The saying goes: "An ocean never dries up",
but we know that your grace also never fails.
Dear Lord, your grace is our happiness. Hallelujah!

A prayer from West Africa

For your own notes

Gabon, Congo and Equatorial Guinea

The populations of *Gabon* and the *Congo*, former French colonies which became part of French Equatorial Africa in 1910, include a substantial number of Christians, particularly Roman Catholics.

Gabon, with a population of 800,000, has about 235,000 Catholics and 100,000 Protestants. Catholic missionaries arrived in 1844 and, for a long period, restricted their work to the coastal region. The first Gabonese priest was ordained in 1899, the hierarchy established in 1955 and the first Gabonese bishop consecrated in 1961. The first Protestant missionaries arrived in 1842. The Paris Missionary Society was particularly active here. Among its centres, the best known is the one in Lambaréné on the Ogoué river where, for almost half a century, the minister, doctor and musicologist Albert Schweitzer directed a hospital which won wide renown. For some years now, the Evangelical Church of Gabon has been split into two groups following internal disputes. The church is a member of the Evangelical Community for Apostolic Action (CEVAA).

The *People's Republic of the Congo* has a population of 1,100,000 made up of Catholics, Protestants, Salvationists, Kimbanguists and also Muslims and Animists. Catholic missionaries arrived in 1883. The first Congolese priest was ordained in 1895, when there were less than 2,000 baptized Catholics. From 1909 the Swedish Evangelical Mission was active in this whole area, at that time called Congo-Brazza.

The Evangelical Church of the Congo has a membership of 50,000. It joined with the Roman Catholic Church, the Salvation Army and the Kimbanguist Church to form the Ecumenical Council of Churches in the Congo.

The life of Christians in former Spanish Guinea, independent since 1968 under the name of *Equatorial Guinea*, is particularly difficult. Living under a dictatorship, the 300,000 inhabitants, 90% of whom are Roman Catholics, have little means of openly professing their faith. Many people have fled the country as refugees. In 1975 all private schools were closed; churches were converted into arms warehouses and public markets; pastors and priests were persecuted.

Evangelical Church of the Congo
Evangelical Church of Equatorial Guinea
Evangelical Church of Gabon
Roman Catholic Church in Congo-Brazzaville, Gabon and Equatorial Guinea
Salvation Army

Include in your prayers all ecumenical councils and working groups at local or national level

Remember also all Christian movements and communities which seek to proclaim and serve Jesus Christ

For Prayer and Intercession

Give thanks . . . that the Gospel has found a home among the people of those countries;
for signs of reconciliation between divided Christians.

Pray . . . that the churches may hear clearly and obey courageously Christ's call to witness to his sovereign love;
that divisions among Christians, inherited and recent, may be overcome;
for refugees and those who labour to help them;
that those who suffer persecution may be sustained by the hope and the joy of the Gospel.

Prayer . . . Lord of lords, Creator of all things, God of all things,
God over all gods, God of sun and rain,
You created the earth with a thought and us with
Your breath.
Lord, we brought in the harvest. The rain watered the earth,
the sun drew cassava and corn out of the clay. Your mercy
showered blessing after blessing over our country. Creeks
grew into rivers; swamps became lakes. Healthy fat cows
graze on the green sea of the savanna. The rain smoothed
out the clay walls, the mosquitoes drowned in the high
waters.
Lord, the yam is fat like meat, the cassava melts on the tongue,
oranges burst in their peels, dazzling and bright.
Lord, nature gives thanks, Your creatures give thanks.
Your praise rises in us like the great river.
Lord of lords, Creator, Provider, we thank you
in the name of Jesus Christ.   Amen.

A prayer from West Africa

For your own notes

Week 10

Zaïre, Rwanda, Burundi and Angola

From the time of Stanley's exploration of the Congo Basin in 1878, Christianity spread rapidly in the heart of black Africa. During the period of the Belgian Congo (independent since 1960, now the Republic of *Zaïre*), the Roman Catholic Church played a predominant role, today embracing more than 40 % of the population. Current concerns include experiments with new forms of pastoral work and with the Africanization of the liturgy and theology.

Other churches in Zaïre originate mostly from work carried out since 1878 by some 43 missionary societies from Britain, North America and Scandinavia. The creation of the Congo Protestant Council in 1928 resulted from early efforts at cooperation among the various missions. In 1970 the Church of Christ in Zaïre was formed, bringing together 53 Protestant communities.

There are several independent churches, the largest being the Church of Christ on Earth by the Prophet Simon Kimbangu. In Zaïre and five neighbouring countries, this church has roughly 5 million faithful and exists chiefly by its own resources without outside aid. In 1959 the colonial authorities at last granted it official recognition and today, with the Roman Catholic Church and the Church of Christ in Zaïre, it is one of the three national Christian churches officially recognized.

For many years, the schools were run by the missionaries and then by Christian churches and communities. Recently, an agreement was made between the churches and the government establishing the responsibilities of each in the area of education.

Rwanda and Burundi are relatively small countries tucked between Zaïre in the west and Tanzania in the east. They became independent republics in 1962 and 1966 respectively. As a result of ethnic and political strife, there is a considerable refugee problem. Densely populated, the countries are faced with severe economic problems. The Roman Catholic Church is by far the largest (50 % of the population). Among the Protestant minority the Anglicans and Baptists are the most active.

Four hundred years ago the Portuguese came to *Angola* and kept it under their occupation until 11 November, 1975, when the country became autonomous after 14 years of war. With the Portuguese came Roman Catholic missionaries. As a result of their work roughly half of the 6 million Angolans are considered Catholic. Protestant missionaries first came to Angola in the 19th century. Today one out of five Angolans belongs to a Protestant church. In 1977, seven churches agreed to form the Angolan Council of Evangelical Churches. The main problems to be faced are: helping scattered congregations and groups in their Christian witness; training leaders, educators and pastors; helping returning refugees and displaced people to settle again; and creating and coordinating programmes and projects which will enable their members to live up to the challenges of independent Angola.

Angola Baptist Convention
Baptist Unions of Rwanda and Burundi
Christian Evangelical Church in Angola
Church of the Brethren in Angola
Church of Christ on Earth by the Prophet Simon Kimbangu
Church of Christ in Zaïre
Church of the Province of Uganda, Rwanda and Burundi
Council of Evangelical Churches in Angola
Evangelical Church in Angola
Evangelical Church of North Angola
Evangelical Church of Zaïre
Evangelical Presbyterian Church in Rwanda
Free Methodist Church – Rwanda and Burundi
Roman Catholic Church in Angola and Sao Tomé
Roman Catholic Church in Zaïre, Rwanda and Burundi
Salvation Army
United Methodist Church in Angola
United Methodist Church – Zaïre and Angola

Include in your prayers all ecumenical councils and working groups at local or national level

Remember also all Christian movements and communities which seek to proclaim and serve Jesus Christ

For Prayer and Intercession

Give thanks . . .   that early efforts at cooperation between the churches continue to bear fruit in the ecumenical movement today;
that conflicts arising from colonial occupation and ethnic tensions have been ended;
that the churches are seeking to make their contributions to the process of nation-building.

Pray . . .   for leaders of the churches, and all engaged in teaching the faith, that they find authentic ways of witnessing to Christ in their present social context;
for those who have suffered in recent conflicts, and those who have inflicted suffering on others, that all may know the grace of forgiveness and healing;
for the churches' ministry to refugees and displaced people.

Prayer . . .   Lord,
we thank you
that our churches
are like big families.
Lord,
let your Spirit of reconciliation
blow over all the earth.
Let Christians live your love.
Lord,
we praise you with Europe's cathedrals,
with America's offerings
and with our African songs of praise.
Lord,
we thank you
that we have brothers in all the world.
Be with them that make peace.

A prayer from West Africa

For your own notes

Week 11

Kenya, Uganda and Tanzania

These three countries have much in common. Their shared interests were symbolized in the formation of the East Africa Community organization, which has now disintegrated.

Kenya and Uganda were colonized by Britain. Tanzania was a German colony (as Tanganyika) until the end of the First World War, when it came under British mandate. Zanzibar, its other component, was a British protectorate.

Since obtaining political independence in the early 1960's, each nation has evolved in a different direction. Kenya has experienced steady economic growth under the leadership of President Kenyatta. President Nyerere has led Tanzania through the "ujamaa" form of socialism. The attention of the world focused recently on Uganda, which saw a radical change of leadership when the military took over in 1971. Under President Amin, Uganda has suffered severely in political, economic, and human terms, and many of its people have died or fled the country.

Christianity in the modern era dates from the last century. There were, however, earlier Christian communities on the east coast which failed to survive. The presence of the Church is due to the work of mission societies from the countries which colonized the area and in latter years others also. There are Orthodox churches in Kenya and Uganda.

African religion was deeply entrenched in all areas of life, and Muslim communities were established before the arrival of Christian missionaries. The Christian community grew rapidly, however, in part due to the African religious interest and the nature of the traditional religions of the people. The Church is strong in Eastern Africa today. Christians number about 68 % of the population of Kenya, about 72 % in Uganda, and about 46 % in Tanzania. Other religious communities include adherents of Islam, African religions, Hinduism, Sikhism and Baha'i.

The witness of the Christian community has not been without cost. Martyrs have suffered and died for their faith in all three countries, and their number has not ceased to grow. The first black Africans canonized as martyrs by the Roman Catholic Church were among the hundreds of Catholics and Anglicans put to death in 1886 at Namugongo, Uganda. In February 1977, Archbishop Janani Luwum of the (Anglican) Church of Uganda was murdered, and many other Christians subsequently have been killed or forced to flee from Uganda.

African Christian Church and Schools, Kenya
African Church of the Holy Spirit
African Israel Church, Nineveh
Baptist Conventions of Kenya and Tanzania
Church of the Province of Kenya
Church of the Province of Tanzania
Church of the Province of Uganda, Rwanda and Burundi
Evangelical Lutheran Church in Tanzania
Greek Orthodox Patriarchate of Alexandria
Lutheran Church of Kenya
Methodist Church in Kenya
Presbyterian Church of East Africa
Reformed Church of East Africa
Roman Catholic Church of Kenya, Tanzania and Uganda
Salvation Army
Society of Friends

Include in your prayers all ecumenical councils and working groups at local or national level

Remember also all Christian movements and communities which seek to proclaim and serve
Jesus Christ

For Prayer and Intercession

Pray . . .

(National affairs)
for the leaders of the three countries; for peace and justice in the area and on its borders;
for Uganda that harmony may be restored, human life respected and security of life and property assured;
for Tanzania that "ujamaa" socialism may bring meaningful rewards to the people, in physical, social and political terms;
for Kenya that peaceful development may continue and that all the people may share in the material welfare of the country.
(Church affairs)
for theological education, in the training of pastors, priests and lay leaders;
for church union discussions in Kenya and Tanzania; and for the three Christian councils;
for evangelistic work that bears witness to the Christian faith;
for international Christian bodies based in Kenya, especially the All Africa Conference of Churches, the Association of Evangelicals of Africa and Madagascar, the Association of the Episcopal Conferences in Eastern Africa, and the World Student Christian Federation (Africa Region).

Prayer . . .

Almighty God, merciful Father who hast commanded intercessions to be made for all men,
we pray thee to direct thy holy Church, that it may abide and grow in unity and in its witness throughout the world, and that our faith may increase.
Grant, we beseech thee, that we may dwell in peace and have thy blessing in our work. Give grace to our government, that it may lead us aright, and that evil may not overtake us.
Be thou the helper of all in need, sickness and distress. Grant that, together with all who have departed in the Lord (especially . . .), we may rejoice in the glory of thy heavenly kingdom. Grant these things, O Father, for the sake of Jesus Christ, our Mediator and Advocate.   Amen.

A United Liturgy for East Africa

For your own notes

Madagascar, Mozambique, Malawi, Zambia

The island of *Madagascar*, for over 70 years under French rule, became independent as the Malagasy Republic in 1960. *Mozambique* was under Portuguese domination for nearly 500 years and became independent only in 1975 after a long struggle. *Malawi* and *Zambia*, on the other hand, were British colonies and became independent in 1966 and 1964 respectively.

Accordingly, the missionary work of the churches has followed different paths. Early Roman Catholic missions (Portuguese) in Madagascar, Mozambique and Malawi left no visible lasting results. In the 19th century missionary agencies began their work on a larger scale and since then many churches have come into existence. Half of the 8 million Malagasy people adhere to their traditional faith and the other half belong to Christian churches, of which the Roman Catholic, (United) Church of Jesus Christ in Madagascar, Lutheran and Anglican are the major bodies. Other active groups include Adventists and Pentecostals. Portuguese rule in Mozambique favoured the Catholic Church and Protestant churches have thus remained relatively small. It remains to be seen how the churches' work will be shaped under the conditions of the new independent leadership.

Malawi has roughly 8 million inhabitants. African traditional religions claim the majority of the population. Twenty percent belong to Islam and 1¼ million are Christians. Of these the Roman Catholic Church is the largest single body. The majority of Protestant churches (including Anglican, Methodist, Presbyterian, Disciples, Baptist, Seventh Day Adventist and various evangelical church bodies) work together in the Christian Council of Malawi.

Of the roughly 4.8 million people of Zambia, 25-30% are considered Christian of whom 60% are Catholic. The various Protestant churches cooperate in the Christian Council of Zambia.

Church union negotiations are under way in Mozambique, Malawi and Zambia. Some pressing problems for the people in these countries stem from the fact that they are border states with Zimbabwe/Rhodesia and the Republic of South Africa. Tensions there have a deep impact. The care for refugees is a major task for churches that are heavily involved in evangelistic, educational, medical and other social work.

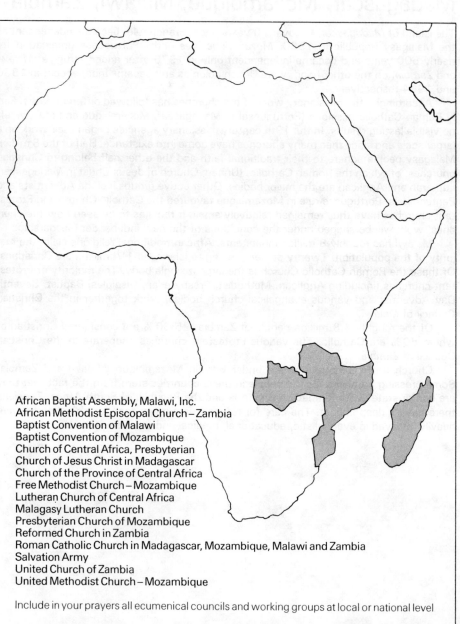

African Baptist Assembly, Malawi, Inc.
African Methodist Episcopal Church – Zambia
Baptist Convention of Malawi
Baptist Convention of Mozambique
Church of Central Africa, Presbyterian
Church of Jesus Christ in Madagascar
Church of the Province of Central Africa
Free Methodist Church – Mozambique
Lutheran Church of Central Africa
Malagasy Lutheran Church
Presbyterian Church of Mozambique
Reformed Church in Zambia
Roman Catholic Church in Madagascar, Mozambique, Malawi and Zambia
Salvation Army
United Church of Zambia
United Methodist Church – Mozambique

Include in your prayers all ecumenical councils and working groups at local or national level

Remember also all Christian movements and communities which seek to proclaim and serve Jesus Christ

For Prayer and Intercession

Give thanks . . .   for all who in these countries have shared in the struggle for justice and reconciliation and contributed to the building of their nations;
for Christians who have been martyred for their witness to God's partisanship with the oppressed, the poor, the forgotten.

Pray . . .   for the unity of divided Christians, and specifically for the union negotiations now under way in Zambia, Malawi and Mozambique;
for the efforts of the churches in the fields of evangelism, education, healing and refugee assistance.

Prayer . . .   O Lord, our Lord, who hast decided that all men, whatever their colour or race, are equal before thee: break down the hatred between men, especially hatred due to national differences. We ask thee to help those in whose hands are the various governments of the world. Reconcile them to one another, so that each may respect the rights of the other.
We ask all this in the name of our Saviour, Jesus Christ.
Student Christian Movement of Zambia

For your own notes

Week 13

Namibia and Zimbabwe

Namibia, originally colonized by Germany, became a mandated territory of the League of Nations after the First World War. Administered since then by South Africa, under the name of South-West Africa, it has been subjected to the apartheid policy of its powerful neighbour. Efforts by the United Nations and liberation movements to end South Africa's control over Namibia's 900,000 people continue, and resulting tensions and governmental pressures still afflict the churches.

The London Missionary Society and an English Methodist mission began work in the area in 1814, but without much visible success. German Protestants from the Rhenish Mission arrived in 1842 and gradually absorbed the work of their predecessors. The Finnish Missionary Society launched operations in the north of the country in 1870. Church growth was hindered by wars and uprisings, including the disruption caused by two world wars, but even so Christians are now estimated at some 87 % of the population.

Lutherans constitute more than half Namibia's Christians. Other major denominations in the area include Roman Catholics, Dutch Reformed and Anglicans. In recent years, attempts to stand against the oppressive policies of the administering power have resulted in such measures as the imprisoning of pastors, the expulsion of foreign mission personnel and the enforced exile of three bishops of the Anglican diocese of Damaraland.

Zimbabwe, formerly the British colony of Southern Rhodesia, has been the scene of escalating military conflict since a white minority regime unilaterally declared independence in 1965.

Christians number about one million of the country's 6$\frac{1}{4}$ million people, the remainder being for the most part followers of African traditional religions. The Gospel arrived in the area along with British commercial and agricultural interests during the latter half of the 19th century. Anglican, Methodist, Congregational, Presbyterian, Lutheran and other churches work together through the Christian Council of Rhodesia.

The two countries have been engaged in a struggle for majority rule in which a number of the churches have played a significant role.

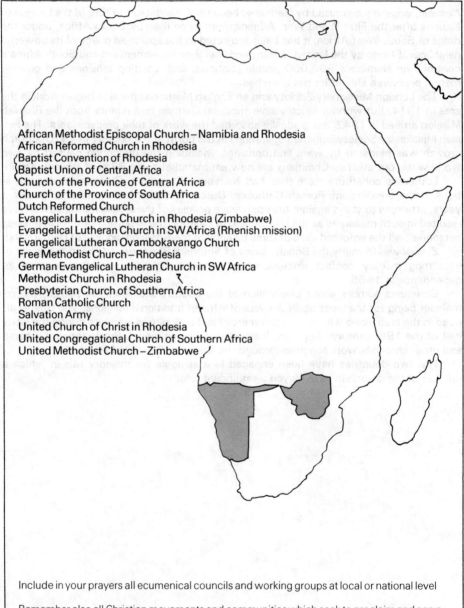

African Methodist Episcopal Church – Namibia and Rhodesia
African Reformed Church in Rhodesia
Baptist Convention of Rhodesia
Baptist Union of Central Africa
Church of the Province of Central Africa
Church of the Province of South Africa
Dutch Reformed Church
Evangelical Lutheran Church in Rhodesia (Zimbabwe)
Evangelical Lutheran Church in SW Africa (Rhenish mission)
Evangelical Lutheran Ovambokavango Church
Free Methodist Church – Rhodesia
German Evangelical Lutheran Church in SW Africa
Methodist Church in Rhodesia
Presbyterian Church of Southern Africa
Roman Catholic Church
Salvation Army
United Church of Christ in Rhodesia
United Congregational Church of Southern Africa
United Methodist Church – Zimbabwe

Include in your prayers all ecumenical councils and working groups at local or national level

Remember also all Christian movements and communities which seek to proclaim and serve Jesus Christ

For Prayer and Intercession

Give thanks . . . for all who with courage and fortitude are bearing witness to Christ as partisan of the oppressed and reconciler of the divided;
for signs of hope and healing evident in both countries.

Pray . . . for all victims of these conflicts, and those whose hearts are torn by bitterness, suspicion and sorrow;
for the churches in the task of nation-building, that they may be symbols of unity, forgiveness and self-giving compassion.

Prayer . . . The Lord is my shepherd;
I have everything I need.
He lets me see a country of justice and peace
and directs my steps towards this land.
He gives me power.
He guides me in the paths of victory,
as he has promised.
Even if a full-scale violent confrontation breaks out
I will not be afraid, Lord,
for you are with me.
Your shepherd's power and love protect me.
You prepare for me my freedom,
where all my enemies can see it;
you welcome me as an honoured guest
and fill my cup with righteousness and peace.
I know that your goodness and love will
be with me all my life
and your liberating love will be my home
as long as I live.

Pastor Kameeta

For your own notes

With our compliments
Avec nos compliments
Mit besten Empfehlungen
Con los atentos saludos

oikoumene

Publications	**World Council of Churches**
Publications	**Conseil Oecuménique des Eglises**
Veröffentlichungen	**Ökumenischer Rat der Kirchen**
Publicaciones	**Consejo Mundial de Iglesias**

P. O. Box No. 66, 150, route de Ferney, 1211 Geneva 20, Switzerland, Tel. (022) 33 34 00

Week 14

South Africa, Botswana, Lesotho and Swaziland

In *South Africa*, a white minority holds the reins of political, economic and military power, exploiting the remaining 5/6 of the population (i.e. about 22 million people) to maintain its position of privilege and affluence. The country, in some ways, represents the world situation in microcosm.

The first denominations arrived in South Africa with the European settlers. Beginning with a chaplaincy function among the new arrivals, their ranks grew to include people of other races. While these "settler" churches are officially multi-racial, congregational life generally reflects the country's ethnic divisions. Residential segregation and language differences are often offered as an explanation. There are, however, notable and important exceptions where mixed congregations function. Dutch Reformed Christians are organized along racial lines.

Other churches began with the initiatives of European and North American missionary societies, and yet others are ethnic enclaves that minister to expatriates from the communities in which they originated. Also, there are numerous independent churches, varying in size and theological orientation. They stem in part from a search for authenticity as seen through black eyes, and to that extent stand in judgement on the historic churches for their lack of Africans in leadership positions and disregard of African cultures.

Church life reflects the tensions, hopes and fears that divide South Africans today. Yet the churches sometimes provide opportunities for mutual understanding, trust and respect and venues for human encounter outside the usual master/servant relationships. Their attempts to witness to the integrity of the Gospel, in the face of the government's claims to be defending "Christian civilization" and its moves to silence all voices of dissent, point to the prospect of a growing clash between Church and state.

Botswana, Swaziland and *Lesotho* achieved political independence from Britain in the 1960's, although economically they remain closely tied to their powerful neighbour, South Africa. The Roman Catholic, Anglican and mainline Protestant denominations are found in all three countries, with Roman Catholics predominant in Lesotho and Congregationalists (formerly London Missionary Society) the largest group in Botswana. Churches here are struggling to produce indigenous leadership, to contribute to nation-building and development and—particularly in Botswana—to respond to the needs of refugees from South Africa, Zimbabwe and Namibia.

African Methodist Episcopal Church
Bantu Presbyterian Church of South Africa
Baptist Union of South Africa
Church of the Province of South Africa
Dutch Reformed Church
Dutch Reformed Church in Africa
Dutch Reformed Church of Africa
Dutch Reformed Mission Church in South Africa
Evangelical Lutheran Church in Southern Africa
Evangelical Lutheran Church in Southern Africa – Cape Church,
    Hermannsburg and Transvaal Church
Free Evangelical Lutheran Synod in Southern Africa
Free Methodist Church
Greek Orthodox (Patriarchate of Alexandria)
Lesotho Evangelical Church
Lutheran Church in Southern Africa
Methodist Church of South Africa
Moravian Church in South Africa
Presbyterian Church of Africa
Presbyterian Church of Southern Africa
Reformed Church in Africa (formerly Indian Reformed)
Roman Catholic Church
Salvation Army
Tsonga Presbyterian Church
United Congregational Church of Southern Africa
Wesleyan Church

Include in your prayers all ecumenical councils and working groups at local or national level

Remember also all Christian movements and communities which seek to proclaim and serve
Jesus Christ

For Prayer and Intercession

Give thanks . . .

for all who by God's grace confess their faith in the Lord Jesus Christ;

for all who struggle in the hope of the liberation which is God's will and his gift to all his children;

for those who continue to hear the Word even when it challenges cherished convictions;

for those who persist in a witness to the Prince of Peace even when perseverance threatens their peace.

Pray . . .

for people who are exploited and oppressed by others;

for people who imprison themselves behind barriers of racism, suspicion and fear;

for those who suffer for faith and conviction and are tempted to turn back because the way is hard;

for refugees and all who seek to minister to them.

Prayers . . .

O God, the Father of all mankind,
we beseech thee so to inspire the people of this land
with the spirit of justice, truth, and love,
that in all our dealings one with another
we may show forth our brotherhood in thee,
for the sake of Jesus Christ our Lord.

A Book Of Common Prayer (South Africa)

God bless Africa!
Guide her leaders, guard her children
and give her peace.

Trevor Huddleston

For your own notes

Iran, Iraq and The States adjoining the Gulf

These countries, despite the presence of the Church since the early centuries, are predominantly Muslim. Recent developments in the oil industry have brought Christians from all over the world, so there may now be as many as 750,000 Christians in the region. The relative freedom which the churches experience varies widely from country to country.

By the 3rd century there were Christians in what is now known as *Iran*. One finds two ancient oriental traditions, the Armenian Episcopal Church with approximately 200,000 faithful, and the Assyrian Church of the East with some 20,000 believers. Some 20,000 Roman Catholics are divided into three rites: Chaldean, Latin and Armenian. The Presbyterian Church in the USA and the Church Missionary Society (England) both continue work they began in the 19th century. The Presbyterian Church is divided into three linguistic groups speaking Persian, Assyrian and Armenian. The Apostolic Church has an episcopal see in Isfahan and approximately 3,000 believers, mostly converts from Islam and Judaism. Expatriates from Europe and North America have recently formed ecumenical community churches.

In addition to 220,000 Roman Catholics mostly of the Chaldean rite, the main Christian groups in *Iraq* are the Assyrian Church of the East, with five dioceses and 170,000 believers, the Syrian Orthodox Church with 20,000 believers and a small Greek Orthodox Church with a bishopric also responsible for Kuwait. The Christian presence in *Kuwait* is only a few decades old but now numbers nearly 50,000 almost all being migrant workers. The Roman Catholic Church and the Greek Orthodox Church are the largest groups, but there is also a lively Evangelical Church, partly stemming from work of the Reformed Church in America. Most of the Oriental traditions are also present.

In *Bahrain*, small evangelical and Roman Catholic communities operate schools. As in other Gulf states, a ministry is carried on though a chain of ecumenically supported family bookshops.

In *Saudi Arabia* some informal chaplaincy work is permitted among the estimated 250,000 expatriate Christians. In the *United Arab Emirates* government facilities and finances have been made available for chaplaincy work among expatriate Christians. The community centres and churches of the Anglican Diocese of Cyprus and the Gulf are examples of this work. For the several thousand Roman Catholics there is an Apostolic Vicar residing at Abu Dhabi.

Building on the foundations of missionary endeavours in hospitals and schools related to the Reformed Church in America, Christians are now cooperating with government officials in *Muscat and Oman*. In *North Yemen*, Roman Catholics are engaged in hospital work at the invitation of the government.

In all these countries Muslims and Christians are challenged to live and work together. In different ways each is indebted to and in need of the other. Barriers of mutual resentment and suspicion for past abuses on both sides must be overcome. Bridges of mutual trust must be built.

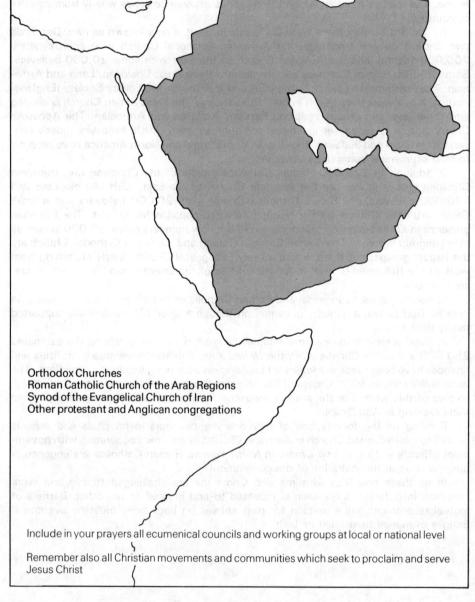

Orthodox Churches
Roman Catholic Church of the Arab Regions
Synod of the Evangelical Church of Iran
Other protestant and Anglican congregations

Include in your prayers all ecumenical councils and working groups at local or national level

Remember also all Christian movements and communities which seek to proclaim and serve Jesus Christ

For Prayer and Intercession

Give thanks . . .
for the churches and Christian groups who have followed Christ in faithful discipleship throughout the centuries;
for all who have given their lives in witness to Jesus Christ in the midst of persecution and hardship;
for all who seek to establish and maintain a Christian presence in countries where other faiths predominate.

Pray . . .
that distrust and hostility between Muslims and Christians give way to mutual respect and openness;
that all people of good will may cooperate so that the great wealth of these lands may be justly shared among all and used for the well-being of humanity.

Prayer . . .
O God, who art the unsearchable abyss of peace,
the ineffable sea of love, the fountain of blessings
and the bestower of affection,
who sendest peace to those that receive it;
Open to us this day the sea of thy love
and water us with plenteous streams
from the riches of thy grace
and from the most sweet springs of thy kindness.
Make us children of quietness and heirs of peace,
enkindle in us the fire of thy love;
sow in us thy fear;
strengthen our weakness by thy power;
bind us closely to thee and to each other
in our firm and indissoluble bond of unity.
Syrian Clementine Liturgy

For your own notes

Turkey, Greece and Cyprus

Since New Testament times the Gospel has been implanted in the lands that are now Turkey, Greece and Cyprus.

Constantinople, now called Istanbul, was next to Rome the greatest centre of the Christian faith for many centuries. Capital of the Byzantine Empire until the 15th century, it succumbed to the pressures of neighbouring peoples and the great strength of Islam.

The great Christian creeds link us with cities like Nicaea or Chalcedon, once great but now almost forgotten. In liturgy or theology, mystic thought or monastic life, Christians still benefit from the work and wisdom of the Church's great teachers who came from this region—Basil and John Chrysostom, Gregory of Nazianzus and Gregory of Nyssa, Maximus the Confessor and Justinian.

Constantinople was the centre around which the Orthodox Church evolved. From there extensive missionary work moved out in many directions, notably to the North and the East. The Ecumenical Patriarchate of Constantinople holds the highest honour and authority for all Orthodox Christians spread over all the continents, regardless of the fact that it is under the constant pressure of Turkish governments. The Ecumenical Patriarchate made a decisive contribution to the ecumenical movement with its famous Encyclical in 1920 calling for closer fellowship between the churches. In Turkey there are also sizable groups of Roman Catholics, Armenians and Syrian Orthodox Christians, but they are a minority in a country which is deeply influenced by Islam. The United Church of Christ in the USA sustains missionary work in Turkey, with an emphasis on educational and medical work.

The Church of *Cyprus* is one of the most ancient churches, founded by Paul and Barnabas. Beginning under the jurisdiction of Antioch, it became independent in the 5th century. There is also a small Roman Catholic minority. The people of Cyprus have gone through a troubled history. Conquered by the Arabs, the Byzantines, the Crusaders, the Venetians, the Turks and the English in the course of the centuries, they are now unhappily divided in two parts, one leaning towards Greece, the other towards Turkey.

The Orthodox Church of *Greece* dates back to St. Paul. Through the ages it has deeply influenced the development of the Greek nation and its liberation from Turkish domination which lasted for almost 400 years. Monastic life has made a deep impact, exemplified by the autonomus "Republic of Monks on Mount Athos" which has existed now for over 1000 years. Independent since 1833, and closely linked with the state, the Orthodox Church of Greece with 8.5 million members is the major religious force in the country. There are small Roman Catholic, Armenian and Protestant churches which, like the Orthodox, find their life and witness challenged by growing secularization.

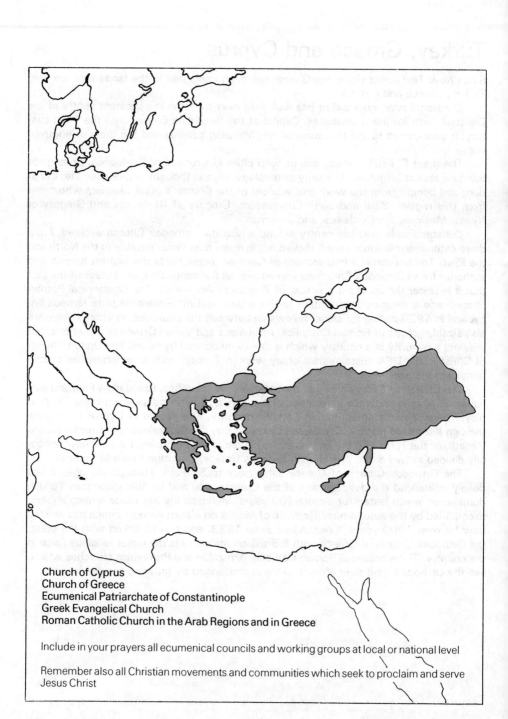

Church of Cyprus
Church of Greece
Ecumenical Patriarchate of Constantinople
Greek Evangelical Church
Roman Catholic Church in the Arab Regions and in Greece

Include in your prayers all ecumenical councils and working groups at local or national level

Remember also all Christian movements and communities which seek to proclaim and serve
Jesus Christ

For Prayer and Intercession

Give thanks . . .	for all the martyrs, saints and teachers of the Church and their heritage; for their wisdom and leadership, their missionary zeal and patient suffering.

Pray . . .	for the unity of the Orthodox Church and the preparations for a Pan-Orthodox Council; for lasting peace between Greeks and Turks, and for a peaceful unity of the people of Cyprus; for ecumenical progress in Greece, with deepened mutual understanding between Christians of different traditions and fruitful collaboration between the churches.

Prayers . . .

Remember, O Lord, thy whole Church;
all who join with us in prayer, all our brethren,
who stand in need of thy grace and succour.
Pour out upon them the riches of thy mercy,
so that we with them, redeemed in soul and body,
and steadfast in faith,
may ever praise thy wonderful and holy name;
through Jesus Christ our Lord.

Early Greek Liturgy—adapted

O Lord, who dost bless them that bless thee,
and hallowest them that put their trust in thee:
save thy people and bless thine inheritance:
preserve the fullness of thy Church:
sanctify them that love the beauty of thy house:
do thou by thy divine power exalt them unto glory,
and forsake us not, who put our trust in thee.
Give peace to thy world, to thy churches,
to the clergy, to our land and to all thy people.
For every good gift is from above,
and cometh down from thee, the Father of lights;
and we give glory, worship and thanks unto thee,
the Father, the Son, and the Holy Spirit,
now and for ever, and world without end.

Liturgy of St. John Chrysostom

For your own notes

Bulgaria, Romania, Yugoslavia and Albania

In these countries, except Albania, the Orthodox churches embrace a majority of the population across a wide range of ethnic groups. Christianity can be traced back to the early centuries. For many centuries the Church was the main force in the defence of national unity, freedom and culture. Today the socialist states which emerged in the Balkans after World War II have established a clear separation between Church and state.

In *Albania* the atheistic character of the state has been so accentuated as to suppress relentlessly the Christian and the Muslim faiths. Formerly, two thirds of the Albanian people were Muslims and one third Christians.

In *Bulgaria* the Orthodox Church dates back to the 9th century. Its patriarchate has been abolished and restored several times. In the course of the liberation struggle against the Turks, the Orthodox Church managed to establish its independent status, resulting in a schism with Constantinople that was finally healed only in 1945. In 1949 the National Assembly recognized the Orthodox Church as separate from the state, but said "the traditional church of the Bulgarian people is inseparable from their history". In a population of 8 million, 6 million belong to the Orthodox Church. There are approximately 720,000 Muslims. The Roman Catholic Church and Protestant churches are small minorities.

The Orthodox Church in Romania forms the only church of a Latin people within the Orthodox world. Christianity dates back to the beginning of the 2nd century. It has always been closely identified with the life of the people and has played a key role in preserving national identity. The Romanian Orthodox Church, while autocephalous, takes care to maintain traditional links with the other Orthodox churches. According to an old tradition, representatives of the Romanian Orthodox Church and of other churches and religious communities are members of the "United Front for Socialism". The state supports church work by annual grants and assists with the restoration and conservation of historical monuments which belong to the church. The Orthodox Church has about 12,500 priests for 14 million faithful. The Roman Catholic minority is mainly of Hungarian origin, living for the most part in Transsylvania. This is also the main area where the Churches of the Reformation are found; the Reformed, Lutheran and Unitarian with 1,000,000, 200,000 and 100,000 members, respectively. The Baptist congregations with 200,000 members are spread across the country. A small number of Romanians are Jews or Muslims.

In *Yugoslavia* the Serbian Orthodox Church has about 8 million members. Church and state were separated in 1953, ending an alliance that dated back to the 13th century when the Serbian princes embraced the newly autonomous Orthodox Church as a national institution. There are some 6 million Roman Catholics, located principally in Croatia and Slovenia. For some years Yugoslavia, together with Poland, has been the only European socialist country to send mission personnel to churches of the Third World.

Baptist Unions of Bulgaria, Romania and Yugoslavia
Bulgarian Orthodox Church
Evangelical Church (Augsburg Confession), Romania
Evangelical Church (Augsburg Confession) in Slovenia
Evangelical Church in the Socialist Republic of Croatia, Bosnia and Herzegovina,
   and in the autonomous province of Vojvodina
Evangelical Synodal Presbyterian Church (Augsburg Confession) in Romania
Reformed Church in Yugoslavia
Reformed Church in Romania
Roman Catholic Church
Romanian Orthodox Church
Serbian Orthodox Church
Slovak Evangelical Christian Church (Augsburg Confession) in Yugoslavia
Slovak Evangelical Church (Augsburg Confession), Yugoslavia
Union of Evangelical Congregational Churches in Bulgaria
United Methodist Church – Bulgaria and Yugoslavia

Include in your prayers all ecumenical councils and working groups at local or national level

Remember also all Christian movements and communities which seek to proclaim and serve
Jesus Christ

For Prayer and Intercession

Give thanks . . .   for the generations of faithful followers of Christ in Albania, Bulgaria, Romania and Yugoslavia, for their teachers and leaders, for the saints and martyrs, unknown and known, throughout the ages;
for the untiring love and witness of the churches in these lands in the midst of opposing world views and faiths.

Pray . . .   for understanding, respect and unity within and between the churches;
for the advance of ecumenical commitment and sharing;
for faithful service to all people in the promotion of justice and peace;
for steadfast witness to Jesus Christ, the Light of the world.

Prayer . . .   O Lord, whose holy saints and martyrs in all times and places have endured affliction, suffering and tribulation, by the power of the Holy Cross, the armour of salvation: so likewise, we pray, send your Holy Spirit, the Comforter and Advocate of all Christians, to sustain these churches in their martyrdom, witness and mission. The world without provocation hates your Church, but you have taught us not to despair. Therefore, you who are a God at hand and not a God afar off, grant to these Christians the power to lift up their hands, their eyes and their hearts to continue their living witness in unity with the universal Church, to the glory of your most holy name.

A prayer of a contemporary Christian from Romania

For your own notes

Italy, Austria and Malta

All three countries are predominantly Roman Catholic in faith and culture.

The Christian faith came to *Italy* and to Rome, the capital of the Roman empire, by humble and unknown believers in the early years of the Christian era. Later they were joined by apostles. Rome became the centre of western Christianity. The contribution of martyrs, teachers and artists throughout almost 2000 years is impossible to enumerate. The spiritual decay and the worldly aspirations of the Roman Church at the end of the Middle Ages were among the principal reasons for the Protestant Reformation. There were earlier movements of reform which survived heavy persecutions. One of these began in the 12th century and led to the formation of the Waldensian Evangelical Church, which in the 16th century associated itself with the Reformation.

Today, with 99% of its people baptized and 82% confirmed, Italy can be considered one of the countries where sacramental involvement is highest. However, participation in worship varies in different regions and social strata. The Roman Catholic Church has a major institutional presence, and over 15,000 Italians are working overseas as priests or in religious orders. The diocese of Rome, which embraces the Vatican City, is headed by the Pope and includes the executive agencies of the Holy See.

The Protestant churches cooperate in a Federation of Evangelical Churches. Many suffered persecution and some form of hostility until two decades ago, but following Vatican II the Roman Catholic Church entered more and more fully into the area of ecumenical cooperation. Groups of Catholics and Protestants engage in common Bible study and action at the local level.

At the time of the Reformation, Protestant churches spread widely in *Austria*. However, the Counter-Reformation brought about decades of heavy persecution. The year 1781 saw the proclamation of the Edict of Toleration which led to the recognition of the remaining small communities of Lutherans and Reformed. Today, the Evangelical Church of the Augsburg and the Helvetic Confession (some 400,000 members) together with the Orthodox, Armenian, Syrian, Anglican, Methodist and Old Catholic churches, form the Ecumenical Council of Churches in Austria, in which the Roman Catholic Church has observer status.

In *Malta* most people are baptized in the Roman Catholic Church which still represents a very powerful institutional force. Hundreds of priests and nuns serve in foreign countries.

Baptist Unions of Austria
Evangelical Church of the Augsburg and Helvetic Confession
Evangelical Lutheran Church in Italy
Evangelical Methodist Church of Italy
Old Catholic Church of Austria
Roman Catholic Church
Salvation Army
Union of Evangelical Christian Baptists of Italy
United Methodist Church – Austria
Waldensian Evangelical Church

Include in your prayers all ecumenical councils and working groups at local or national level

Remember also all Christian movements and communities which seek to proclaim and serve Jesus Christ

For Prayer and Intercession

Give thanks . . .

for the presence of the Christian churches in these lands for almost 2000 years;

for the expression of the faith through ancient and modern art;

for the new ecumenical relationships and initiatives made possible through the Second Vatican Council, in a rediscovered faithfulness to the Word of God.

Pray . . .

for the churches in these countries, their mutual openness and cooperation, their renewal and dedication;

for those who in these churches carry heavy responsibilities, that they may have wisdom to discern and courage to obey God's will;

for Pope John Paul and the Curia of the Roman Catholic Church;

for the people in Italy, Malta and Austria, and their engagement in the struggle for justice, peace and freedom in mutual respect.

Prayers . . .

Almighty and everlasting God, you gather together your scattered children: look upon the sheep of your Son's flock, that as they have been consecrated by the one baptism they may be drawn together in integrity of faith and united in the bond of love;

through Jesus Christ, your Son our Lord, who reigns with you and the Holy Spirit, now and for ever.

Roman Missal, 'Mass for the Unity of the Church'

Lord, make us instruments of your peace.
> Where there is hatred, let us sow love;
> where there is injury, pardon;
> where there is discord, union;
> where there is doubt, faith;
> where there is despair, hope;
> where there is darkness, light;
> where there is sadness, joy.

Grant that we may not seek so much to be comforted
> as to comfort;
> to be understood as to understand;
> to be loved as to love;
> for it is in giving that we receive;
> it is in forgiving that we are forgiven,
> and it is in dying that we are born into
> eternal life; through Jesus Christ our Lord.

St. Francis of Assisi

For your own notes

France and Switzerland

By the end of the 1st century Christians were gathering in southern *France* for worship. Despite persecutions the new faith spread in the main centres of Roman settlement, and subsequently the missionary endeavours of Irish monks played a significant role. The life of the Church, its missionary and social activities, theological study and artistic work, centred largely around monasteries and cathedrals. Religious and political aspirations split the unity of mediaeval Christendom at the time of the Reformation. Under the leadership of Calvin and Bucer, Protestantism became a strong force in France, but severe persecutions reduced it to a small minority (today some 800,000 Reformed and Lutherans).

Some 80 % of the French are baptized Catholics, but only 15 % participate in the life of the Church. In response to this situation, new forms of mission and ministry are being developed, lay movements are being encouraged, theologians and philosophers are helping the churches to come to grips with the contemporary intellectual and spiritual climate, and Vatican II initiatives in the fields of biblical, liturgical and catechetical renewal are making themselves felt in parish life. Muslims now outnumber Protestants as the second largest religious community in France.

The presence of Christians in *Switzerland* dates back to the 4th century. In the centuries following, the monasteries of St. Gallen and Einsiedeln became influential centres of learning and mission. The 16th century Reformation had a stronghold in Switzerland, especially in Zürich, through Zwingli and Bullinger and notably in Geneva where John Calvin deeply influenced the development of Protestantism. In about half the Swiss cantons large Reformed churches came into existence, while the Roman Catholic Church remained strong in the "Catholic" cantons. Since the end of the 19th century, the much smaller Old Catholic Church has been recognized by the state as a third official Christian confession. There are also several small free churches.

Population mobility has contributed both to far-reaching secularization and also to shifts in the religious pattern of the country. Roman Catholics, for example, are growing in numbers and in 1970 became the largest confessional group. Such mobility has also helped pave the way for a closer collaboration between Protestants and Catholics. The churches are still generally respected as useful religious institutions. However, although majority churches intimately linked with the political, social and economic structures of their society find it difficult to fulfil a prophetic ministry, nevertheless new insights and initiatives have come from these old churches in their efforts to be Christ's Church in the contemporary world.

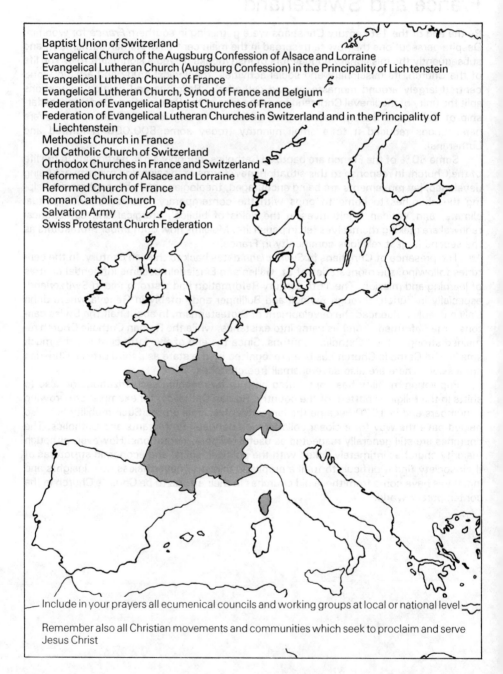

Baptist Union of Switzerland
Evangelical Church of the Augsburg Confession of Alsace and Lorraine
Evangelical Lutheran Church (Augsburg Confession) in the Principality of Lichtenstein
Evangelical Lutheran Church of France
Evangelical Lutheran Church, Synod of France and Belgium
Federation of Evangelical Baptist Churches of France
Federation of Evangelical Lutheran Churches in Switzerland and in the Principality of
    Liechtenstein
Methodist Church in France
Old Catholic Church of Switzerland
Orthodox Churches in France and Switzerland
Reformed Church of Alsace and Lorraine
Reformed Church of France
Roman Catholic Church
Salvation Army
Swiss Protestant Church Federation

Include in your prayers all ecumenical councils and working groups at local or national level

Remember also all Christian movements and communities which seek to proclaim and serve
Jesus Christ

For Prayer and Intercession

Give thanks . . .
for the presence of Christ's Church in the villages and cities of France and Switzerland during almost twenty centuries; for the many saints, thinkers, artists and "fools for Christ's sake" who in these countries have glorified God through their life and work.

Pray . . .
for the sanctification of Christians in these countries where material abundance tends to stifle the courage of faith; for pastors and lay people that they may give clear testimony to Jesus Christ among the many young and old, who search for a meaning for their lives amidst the emptiness of a consumer society; for the unity of the Church, the fellowship of Christians in each place and the united witness in social and political concerns.

Prayers . . .
O Father everlasting, the light of faithful souls, who didst bring the nations to thy light and kings to the brightness of thy rising: fill the world with thy glory, we beseech thee, and show thyself unto all the nations; through him who is the true light and the bright and morning star, Jesus Christ, thy Son, our Lord.

Gothic Missal

O Lord, our God; you humbled yourself that we might be exalted. You became poor that we might be enriched. You came to us that we might come to you. You became a man like us that we might share in eternal life. All this was done by virtue of your free grace which we have not deserved, and through your Son, our Lord and Saviour Jesus Christ.

Karl Barth

For your own notes

Week 20

Portugal and Spain

According to an old tradition, St. Paul himself preached the Gospel in Spain. In the early Church, Christianity in the Iberian peninsula played an important role—for example, in the actual wording of the Apostles' Creed.

A long period of Muslim influence left deep traces in the culture and the expressions of faith of Iberian Christians. The late middle ages not only gave Spain an important world role but also laid the foundations for the Church's outreach in the extensive Spanish colonial empire. The 16th and 17th centuries, with people like Ignatius Loyola (founder of the Jesuits) and Francis Xavier (missionary to Asia), were notable for enduring contributions to theology, mission and spirituality. The Protestant Reformation found roots in both countries but a decisive counter-movement suppressed it completely. It was not before the middle of the 19th century that a variety of Protestant missionary activities were deployed on the Iberian peninsula, resulting in a number of small, independent and sometimes sectarian denominations.

In more recent times, the fascist dictatorships which lasted in both countries for decades marked the life and witness of the churches deeply. Protestants had to struggle for their own survival. The Roman Catholic Church in Spain was better prepared for the transition to democracy than was its Portuguese opposite number. The latter, polarized by the country's political situation in general and its African wars in particular, also had been less influenced by the thinking of Vatican II. In both countries some religious orders, local priests, university chaplains and bishops had begun to identify themselves clearly with groups in opposition to government policy.

Recent democratization processes in both countries present new challenges to the Christian communities in the peninsula. Growing industrialization and secularization seem likely to diminish the churches, influence. New ways of diaconal ministries will need to be found as governments assume growing responsibility for education, health and care for the elderly.

The development of ecumenical relations between large established churches and very small minority denominations is never easy, but in both these countries progress is being made. Within the Protestant churches there are discussions about the possibility of greater unity.

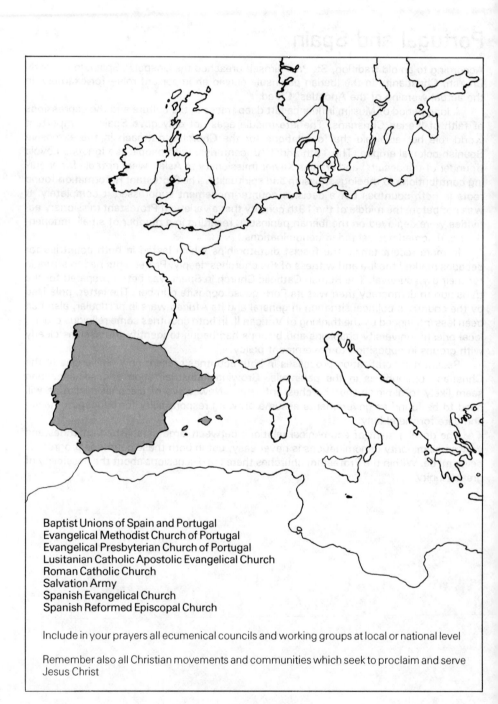

Baptist Unions of Spain and Portugal
Evangelical Methodist Church of Portugal
Evangelical Presbyterian Church of Portugal
Lusitanian Catholic Apostolic Evangelical Church
Roman Catholic Church
Salvation Army
Spanish Evangelical Church
Spanish Reformed Episcopal Church

Include in your prayers all ecumenical councils and working groups at local or national level

Remember also all Christian movements and communities which seek to proclaim and serve Jesus Christ

For Prayer and Intercession

Give thanks . . .
for the many centuries of Christian witness in Spain and Portugal and for the blessings which Christians from these countries have brought to peoples elsewhere;
for new ecumenical beginnings, for forms of collaboration developing between the Christian churches and communities.

Pray . . .
for Christians in these countries, for their mutual openness and trust, for renewal and dedication under the guidance of God's Word;
for unity within and between the churches, both big and small, for the deepening of their ecumenical commitment and their common service to Christ;
for the people of Spain and Portugal, for all who carry heavy responsibilities in government and other sectors of society, for steady and stable development in justice and peace.

Prayers . . .
Let thy mercy, O Lord, be upon us, and the brightness of thy Spirit illumine our inward souls; that he who abideth evermore with thee in glory may kindle our cold hearts and light up our dark minds.

Mozarabic Missal

Teach us, good Lord,
    to serve thee as thou deservest;
    to give and not to count the cost;
    to fight and not to heed the wounds;
    to toil and not to seek for rest;
    to labour and not to ask for any reward,
    save that of knowing that we do thy will;
    through Jesus Christ our Lord.

St. Ignatius Loyola

For your own notes

Week 21

Belgium, Luxembourg and The Netherlands

Christianity came to these countries during the 6th and 7th centuries. Irish missionaries were the first martyrs in the Lowlands. Soon bishoprics were established and important centres of learning, Louvain for example, developed.

What is now *Belgium* has remained predominantly Roman Catholic. Originally, the Reformation was stronger in Flanders than in the north, with the leaders of intellectual and commercial life joining first of all the Lutheran and very soon the Reformed churches. At the time of the Counter-Reformation, in the reign of the Spanish (later Austrian) Hapsburgs, thousands of people were martyred and many fled north. It was only after the Edict of Tolerance was promulgated in the 18th century that the remnants of Protestantism received recognition.

Today in Belgium the Roman Catholic Church baptizes 90% of the population and finds expression in major educational, medical and other social endeavours. The presence of many migrant workers has made Islam the second largest religious community (in the Netherlands it is the third largest). The small Protestant minority has been involved in moves towards unity, and cooperation with the Roman Catholic Church has been growing steadily.

A spirit of tolerance marked the Calvinist churches in the *Netherlands*. Throughout the centuries this country has been a place of refuge for thousands searching for religious and intellectual freedom. A reorganization of the Roman Catholic Church took place in the late 19th century when it was granted the right to appoint bishops, and its struggle for identity was reinforced with the founding of the Roman Catholic University of Nijmegen. There is now a thriving Roman Catholic community that has grown beyond the ghetto spirit that once characterized it and in recent years has taken many initiatives to give expression to the spirit of the Second Vatican Council. The Council of Churches in the Netherlands, in which the Roman Catholic Church has full membership, has become an increasingly important force, and the Dutch churches have given outstanding leadership to the wider ecumenical movement.

Both Belgium and the Netherlands are highly industrialized countries marked by increasing secularization. The churches seek ways of renewing their witness and service in this spiritual milieu.

Luxembourg is predominantly Roman Catholic, but there are a few Protestant congregations. When the headquaters of the European Community was established in Luxembourg City, a lively Protestant ecumenical parish came into existence.

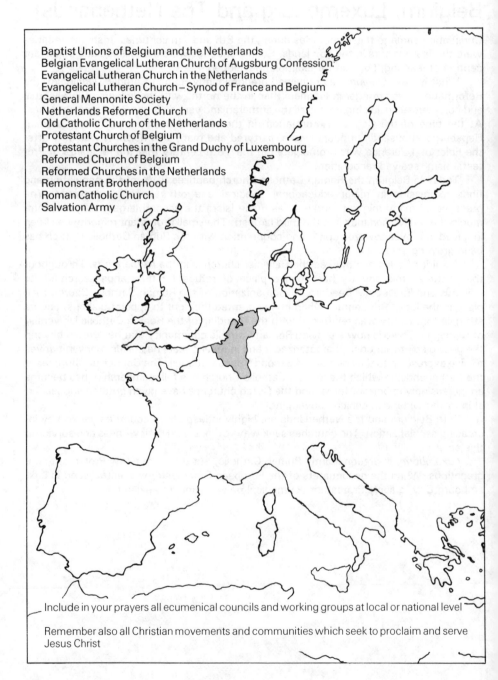

Baptist Unions of Belgium and the Netherlands
Belgian Evangelical Lutheran Church of Augsburg Confession
Evangelical Lutheran Church in the Netherlands
Evangelical Lutheran Church – Synod of France and Belgium
General Mennonite Society
Netherlands Reformed Church
Old Catholic Church of the Netherlands
Protestant Church of Belgium
Protestant Churches in the Grand Duchy of Luxembourg
Reformed Church of Belgium
Reformed Churches in the Netherlands
Remonstrant Brotherhood
Roman Catholic Church
Salvation Army

Include in your prayers all ecumenical councils and working groups at local or national level

Remember also all Christian movements and communities which seek to proclaim and serve Jesus Christ

For Prayer and Intercession

Give thanks . . .

for all the Christians, known and unknown, in the three countries, who have lived out their faith in obedience and discipleship both at home and among many peoples abroad;
for the long tradition of tolerance and renewal in church and society, in theology, mission and spiritual life;
for the courageous initiatives and outstanding leadership of Christians from these countries in the ecumenical movement.

Pray . . .

for the continuation of the vigorous and imaginative efforts to proclaim the Gospel of Christ in an increasingly secularized culture;
that the churches may never waver in the pursuit of unity;
for the leaders of the three countries in all sectors of society, that they may be heralds of peace and doers of justice.

Prayers . . .

Lord Jesus Christ, who hast said that thou art the Way, the Truth and the Life: we pray thee suffer us not at any time to stray from thee, who art the Way; nor ever to distrust thy promises, who art the Truth; nor to rest in any other thing than thee, who art the Life; for thou hast taught us what to believe, what to do, and wherein to rest.

Erasmus

Let us pray for all those, throughout the world, who believe in the Gospel:
That they may grow in grace and humanity.
Let us also pray for all churches, that they may not lay up treasures on earth or become monuments to a past age,
Clinging to what is already dead and remote from people of today,
But that they may be converted and receive the spirit of Jesus, our Lord, who is the light and life, hope and peace of this world, for ever and ever.

Huub Oosterhuis

97

For your own notes

Week 22

Ireland

It is probable that there were Christians in Ireland (ancient Hibernia) by the 4th century. Early in the 5th century, Palladius was sent as bishop to the "Irish believing in Christ". St. Patrick, however, is generally remembered as the evangelist of the island and founder of the Church there. Born in Britain, Patrick was taken to Ireland as a slave, escaped to Gaul and returned to Ireland as bishop in 432 A.D. With the collapse of the Roman civilization, Ireland was relatively isolated from the rest of Christendom and developed its own rich tradition of monastic life and learning, with a vigorous missionary concern which helped spread the Gospel in Scotland and mainland Europe.

It was in the centuries of British hegemony (16th to 20th centuries) and in particular with the "plantation of Ulster" in the 17th century (with its introduction of English and Scottish "planters" in the north) that the seeds of the present political troubles were sown. These planters were mainly Anglican and Presbyterian. The present "two states of Ireland" were born in revolution. After the nationalist rising in Dublin in 1916, a referendum was held and by 1921 partition was a reality. The north remained part of the United Kingdom while the south became independent.

Today the vast majority of the nearly 3 million people in the Republic of Ireland are Roman Catholic, and 30 % of the 1.5 million people in Northern Ireland are Catholic too. Irish Catholicism has had a remarkable role worldwide, and even today some 40 % of its priests are serving in foreign dioceses. The largest of the other churches are the Presbyterian, Church of Ireland, and the Methodist Church. These are concentrated in the north but, like the Roman Catholic Church, they cover the whole of the island.

The political and social scene today is dominated by the problems of the north where there is a bitter political struggle between those who reject a divided Ireland at any price and those who cling to the traditional links with the rest of the United Kingdom at any price. Christians of different confessions who are weary and ashamed of so much bloodshed and disorder, violence and bitterness are yearning for better ways for themselves and their children. A hopeful sign in a context where hopes have often deceived and fears materialized is the peace movement initiated and led by women, both Catholic and Protestant. But the exorcizing of ancient demons and the abandonment of tribal ideologies is recognized as a task requiring much time and patient prayer and action. The churches which have contributed in varying degrees and various ways in the past to today's crisis are beginning to see a common calling in the service of true community.

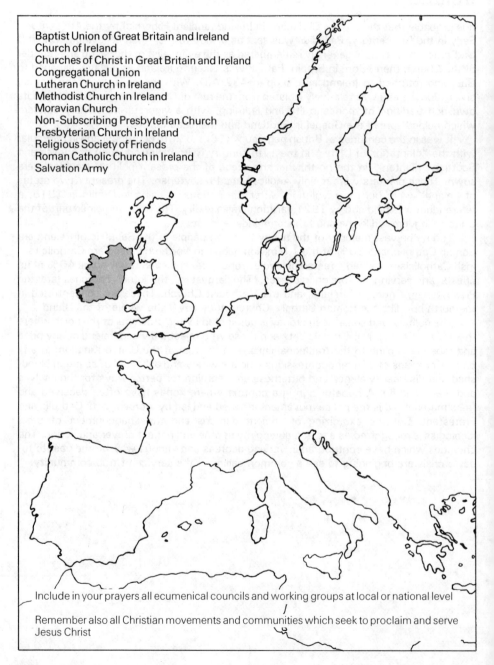

Baptist Union of Great Britain and Ireland
Church of Ireland
Churches of Christ in Great Britain and Ireland
Congregational Union
Lutheran Church in Ireland
Methodist Church in Ireland
Moravian Church
Non-Subscribing Presbyterian Church
Presbyterian Church in Ireland
Religious Society of Friends
Roman Catholic Church in Ireland
Salvation Army

Include in your prayers all ecumenical councils and working groups at local or national level

Remember also all Christian movements and communities which seek to proclaim and serve Jesus Christ

For Prayer and Intercession

Give thanks . . .   for the powerful witness of Irish Christians during the early centuries which brought the Gospel of Jesus Christ to many peoples in Europe;
for the courage of all who are working to heal the wounds of Northern Ireland.

Pray . . .   that all Christians and churches in Ireland may cast aside sectarian interests, rediscover their oneness in Christ and be living witnesses to his reconciling power;
that they may be enabled to look penitently at themselves and thus be set free to serve the wellbeing of all.

Prayer . . .   Father, I am a man of my time and situation.
Around me, the signs and symbols of man's fear,
hatred, alienation;
a bomb exploding in crowded market square;
demagogic faces on TV twisted in mocking confrontation.
It's not that we haven't tried, Father,
to find ways to peace and reconciliation
but always too little, too late;
the forces of opposition were too great.
My hopes have been destroyed.
But the death of things I hoped for has been celebrated
by others as victory in your power, Father.
Can this be so?
I am perplexed, angry, hopeless, sick. I want to turn
my back, wash my hands, save myself, my family, get out.
But every time I turn to go,
there stands in my way a cross . . . .
Lord, make me a child of hope, reborn from apathy,
cynicism, and despair, ready to work for that new man
you have made possible by walking the way of the cross
yourself.
I *do* have hope grounded on your victory over powers
of evil, death itself; focused on your kingdom,
breaking in on us now as light out of deep darkness.
And I do see signs of hope immediately around me
I see a wider sign:
I see a sign—flowers growing on a bombed-out site.
The sign—an empty cross. The burden, Lord, is yours.
Lord, I am a prisoner of hope! There *is* a life before death.

A prayer from Northern Ireland

For your own notes

Week 23

Great Britain

Near 200 A.D. Christians appeared in Roman Britain. When the Roman Empire declined, Britain was overrun. Much of the Church's life, especially in the south, was destroyed. St. Augustine's arrival (end of the 6th century) and the foundations laid by Celtic missionaries in the northern and western parts of Britain, led to the faith spreading to all parts.

Christianity in Britain is largely the outcome of the 16th century Reformation and the religious struggle that ensued. Important later influences have included the Methodist movement (18th century) and the Catholic revival (19th century). The three countries which, with Northern Ireland, make up the United Kingdom, have distinctive church patterns. All have been profoundly affected by 20th-century upheavals and the transition to a post-colonial role. Discussion continues about the best relationships of the nations within the United Kingdom, an issue of far-reaching importance for the churches.

In *England* (population nearly 46 million), the Church of England is the established church with 42 dioceses, led by the Archbishops of Canterbury and York. There are efforts to achieve greater collegiality in government and greater independence from the state, in e.g., the appointment of bishops. Alongside it are the historic Free churches: The Methodists form the largest group, the Baptists the next largest. The United Reformed Church (1972) brought together many Congregationalists and Presbyterians. The Society of Friends with its centuries of work for peace and international understanding and the Salvation Army with its evangelism and service are among the influential religious bodies. There is a strong Roman Catholic Church which owes much to the influx of Irish immigrant workers. The Orthodox churches are in diaspora in many cities.

In *Scotland* (population 5 1/2 million) the national church is the (Presbyterian) Church of Scotland, speaking for a nation religiously more homogeneous than England. The Roman Catholic Church is also strong. A number of small Free churches and the Episcopal Church are also active.

In *Wales* (population 2 3/4 million) there is no single national or established church. The (Episcopal) Church in Wales is strong throughout the principality, as are the Calvinistic Methodists (Presbyterian Church) and the Union of Welsh Independents (Congregational). Welsh Christians are noted for their love of music and song.

For long there have been sizable Jewish communities, and recent migrations have added to the diversity of the religious scene. Among Africans and West Indians there are a number of churches, often Pentecostal in their worship. Among migrants from Asia there are Hindu, Sikh and Muslim (one million) communities.

The British churches have contributed much to the ecumenical movement, through major conferences and outstanding individuals. An effective network of councils of churches, 200 or more ecumenical parishes, and close cooperation in many voluntary bodies point to growing ecumenical awareness.

African Methodist Episcopal Church
African Methodist Episcopal Zion Church
Baptist Union of Great Britain and Ireland
Church of England
Church of Scotland
Church of Wales
Churches of Christ in Great Britain and Ireland
Congregational Union of Scotland
Episcopal Church in Scotland
Evangelical Lutheran Church of England
Lutheran Council of Great Britain
Methodist Church
Moravian Union
Orthodox churches in diaspora
Presbyterian Church of Wales
Roman Catholic Church
Salvation Army
Society of Friends
Union of Welsh Independents
United Free Church of Scotland
United Reformed Church of England and Wales

Include in your prayers all ecumenical councils and working groups at local or national level

Remember also all Christian movements and communities which seek to proclaim and serve
Jesus Christ

For Prayer and Intercession

Give thanks . . .   for all who have served Christ and his kingdom in Britain and throughout the world since the Gospel was first brought there; for outstanding pioneers in the ecumenical movement and those known only to God, from all Christian traditions, and for all who continue their work in Britain today; for all who seek to promote truth, justice and peace in Britain's multi-racial society.

Pray . . .   that through the diversity and despite the divisions of the British churches the universal Gospel of the love of God in Jesus Christ may be set forth; that the churches may so order their life, witness and service that they may assist the growth of true community and peace among different races and religions; that the churches in Britain may discern more clearly their place today in the worldwide ecumenical movement.

Prayers . . .   O Lord, without whom our labour is but lost, and with whom thy little ones go forth as the mighty; be present to all works in thy Church which are undertaken according to thy will; and grant to thy labourers a pure intention, patient faith, sufficient success upon earth, and the bliss of serving thee in heaven; through Jesus Christ our Lord.

William Bright

O God, the Creator and Preserver of all mankind, we humbly beseech thee for all sorts and conditions of men; that thou wouldest be pleased to make thy ways known unto them, thy saving health unto all nations. More especially, we pray for the good estate of the Catholic Church; that it may be so guided and governed by thy good Spirit, that all who profess and call themselves Christians may be led into the way of truth, and hold the faith in unity of spirit, in the bond of peace, and in righteousness of life. Finally, we commend to thy fatherly goodness all those who are in any ways afflicted or distressed, in mind, body, or estate; that it may please thee to comfort and relieve them, according to their several necessities, giving them patience under their sufferings, and a happy issue out of all their afflictions. And this we beg for Jesus Christ his sake.

Book of Common Prayer

For your own notes

Norway, Sweden, Denmark, Finland and Iceland

Christianity was introduced to the Nordic countries from two different directions: from the British Isles to Western Norway and from Germany/Friesland to Denmark, Sweden and Eastern Norway. Agents of mission were monks, individuals impressed by experiences on Viking voyages and, above all, bishops accompanying their kings on journeys. Ansgar, later Archbishop of Hamburg-Bremen, is known as the apostle of Scandinavia. The first archbishopric (for all Scandinavia) was founded at Lund in 1103. When Norway became a separate country in 1153, the archbishopric of Nidaros (Trondheim) was founded by the English cardinal, Nicholas, who later became Pope Adrian IV. By the end of the 12th century the Church was firmly established in all the Nordic countries.

Orthodoxy began to extend among the Finnish Karelians at the beginning of the second millenium, chiefly as a result of missions by Greek and Russian monks. For centuries this easternmost province of the Finnish tribes formed part of the archbishopric of Novogorod. The leading monastic centre was on the island of Valamo on Lake Ladoga.

The Reformation came to the Nordic countries through a variety of influences. In some cases it was brought back by Nordic students who had studied theology in Germany and were strongly influenced by the views of Luther and Melanchthon. In other cases political and social factors played a dominant role. In general the Reformation proceeded without violence in Scandinavia, though more slowly than in the rest of Europe. By the end of the 16th century it had penetrated all levels of life. Former Catholic dioceses quietly became Lutheran and, ever since, the Lutheran churches have had a majority position in the respective countries.

Although secularization has eroded this traditional status and the Church-state connection has recently been criticized, about 95 % of the population in these countries still adheres, nominally at least, to the national churches. The other 5 % are attached to various Protestant Free churches, the Orthodox Church, the Roman Catholic Church, or to no church at all. The Mission Covenant Church originated in the 19th century, with a strong commitment to mission and a congregationalist polity.

The Orthodox Church of Finland is that country's second national church, although including only 1.2 % of the population. It is autonomous under the spiritual oversight of the Ecumenical Patriarchate of Constantinople. Numerous Orthodox parishes have been established in Sweden in recent years for the spiritual needs of immigrants from Greece, Serbia and other countries.

Partnership in evangelism and service with other European churches led the Nordic churches to participate in the ecumenical movement from the beginning. Many are members of the World Council of Churches and there are ecumenical councils in Sweden, Denmark and Finland organizing cooperation and joint projects.

Baptist Unions of Denmark, Finland, Norway and Sweden
Church of Denmark
Church of Norway
Church of Sweden
Evangelical-Lutheran Church of Finland
Evangelical Lutheran Church of Iceland
Evangelical Lutheran Free Churches of Denmark and Norway
Mission Covenant Churches of Denmark, Finland, Norway and Sweden
Orthodox Church in Finland
Orthodox Church of Greece
Pentecostalist Movement
Reformed Synod of Denmark
Roman Catholic Church
Salvation Army
Swedish Alliance Mission
United Methodist Church – Denmark, Finland, Norway, Sweden

Include in your prayers all ecumenical councils and working groups at local or national level

Remember also all Christian movements and communities which seek to proclaim and serve Jesus Christ

For Prayer and Intercession

Give thanks . . .
for the long centuries of courageous and creative witness by Nordic Christians, both at home and abroad;
for the pioneering leadership of many from these countries in the ecumenical movement.

Pray . . .
for family life, the strengthening of marriage, the growth of trusting and sustaining relationships between wife and husband, children and parents;
for Christian education in and outside the public schools;
for the changing relationships between states and churches, that Christ's people may continue to fulfil their mission and service to the world.

Prayer . . .
Lord, we thank thee for all the light and grace and life that thou hast given in that branch of the Church to which we belong . . .
Set us free from error and from narrow self-sufficiency.
Open our eyes that we may recognize the work of thy Spirit among other people and under different forms.
Banish the spirit of division which has so long humiliated and weakened Christendom. Arouse a desire for cooperation and unity. Draw us nearer to thee and thereby lead us nearer to one another. As thou art the Father of all, create in us a steadfast temper of brotherhood. As we are one in the life which thou givest through the same Saviour, unite us also in thought and action. Make us honestly willing to learn from one another, and give us grace to rejoice at another's progress in thy service.
Swedish Lutheran prayer

For your own notes

The German Democratic Republic and the Federal Republic of Germany

The countries in Central Europe where German peoples live have very few natural boundaries, with the result that throughout history these peoples have been accessible to cultural and political influences from all sides. Those who converted the German tribes to Christianity also came from various directions and at various times, first from the old Roman Empire, later from Britain and Ireland. Subsequently, missionaries went from Germany to both north and east. Many elements of German Christianity and culture likewise moved in many directions. The Reformation of Martin Luther is a good example of the former, Marxism of the latter. German theology, philosophy, and music have also at times exerted a considerable influence in much of the world.

World War II led to a partitioning of Germany. In 1949 the larger western part was proclaimed the Federal Republic of Germany and the smaller eastern part declared the German Democratic Republic.

The German Democratic Republic with a population of 17 million is led by the United Socialist Party and strongly linked to the other socialist states in Europe. The churches have made great efforts to cope with their changed status and diminishing membership. They seek actively to witness and serve the people in a Marxist-Leninist society. The eight territorial churches—five United and three Lutheran—and the associated Moravian Church founded the Federation of Evangelical Churches in 1969. It has become an important instrument in the search for unity and church cooperation.

An estimated 50 % of the population still acknowledge church adherence. They are predominantly Protestant. There are more than one million Catholics in six dioceses. The Reformed are a small minority. So are the Methodists, the Baptists, Free Congregations, Independent Lutherans, Mennonites and Old Catholics.

The Federal Republic of Germany has a population of 62 million, including the people of West-Berlin. It is closely linked to the countries adjoining the North Atlantic. Its economic prosperity and wealth has made it an important factor in the worldwide networks of economic dependencies and domination. Roughly half of the people are Protestant, the other Roman Catholic. Most Protestants belong to the established territorial churches with a Lutheran, United or Reformed character. Together they form the Evangelical Church in Germany. Baptists, Methodists as well as Old Catholics and other communities of the Free Church tradition are also present. The presence of millions of migrant workers in the Republic has made the Greek Orthodox Church the third largest Christian group. There are also very small Jewish and Muslim communities.

The Christians in the two German states are faced with very different challenges and are seeking to witness to them in the light of the Gospel in many distinctive ways. These tasks give added weight to ecumenical work which has, on the whole, been actively supported in the German churches. With councils and working groups developing at all levels, ecumenical cooperation is gaining momentum within the countries and beyond.

Federal Republic of Germany
Catholic Diocese of Old Catholics
Evangelical Church in Germany
Evangelical-Old-Reformed Church in Lower Saxony
Federation of Evangelical Free Churches in the FRG (Baptists)
Federation of Free Evangelical Congregations in the FRG (Congregationalists)
Fellowship of Christian Communities (Christlicher Gemeinschaftsverband)
Greek Orthodox Metropoly (Exarchate of Central Europe)
Independent Evangelical-Lutheran Church
Moravian Church
Roman Catholic Church
Salvation Army
Society of Friends (Quakers)
Union of Mennonites
United Methodist Church – FRG Central Conference

German Democratic Republic
Federation of Evangelical Free Churches in the GDR (Baptists)
Federation of Free Evangelical Congregations in the GDR (Congregationalists)
Federation of Old Catholic Churches in the GDR
Independent Evangelical Lutheran Church
Mennonite Community
Moravian Church
Reformed General Council
Roman Catholic Church
United Methodist Church
– GDR Central Conference

Include in your prayers all ecumenical councils and working groups at local or national level

Remember also all Christian movements and communities which seek to proclaim and serve Jesus Christ

For Prayer and Intercession

Give thanks . . .
    for the 16th-century Reformation and its legacy;
for the rich tradition of sound theological learning and research;
for the courage of confessing Christians—pastors and priests, bishops and clergy, lay men and women during the church struggle in the Nazi period;
for the honesty of repentance and reparation in the post-war years and for generosity in support of the ecumenical movement and its programmes.

Pray . . .
    for the churches in the two Republics that they may faithfully bear witness to the hope of the Gospel in their respective situations, encouraging one another and praying for one another;
for Christians in their daily life and work;
for pastors and theologians.

A Prayer for Unity:
    O, eternal and merciful God, you are a God of peace and love and unity—and not of the discord and confusion which, in your righteous judgement, you have permitted to happen. This world has become divided and broken in that it has forsaken you. For you alone can create and sustain unity. In its own wisdom this world has fallen away from you, especially in those things which pertain to your divine truth and to the blessedness of our souls. As in its own so-called wisdom the world comes to shame by its being torn apart, so may it return again to you, who love unity.

We poor sinners, to whom you have graciously granted that we acknowledge this condition, we beseech and implore you: through your Holy Spirit bring together again all that is scattered; unify what is divided; and make it completely whole. Grant therefore that we turn to your unity, seek your truth, and avoid all discord. So may we become of one will, one knowledge, one disposition, one understanding that relies upon Jesus Christ our Lord. In the harmony of unity may we praise and adore you, the heavenly Father of our Lord Jesus Christ. Through him in the Holy Spirit we pray.   Amen.

Martin Luther, 1522

113

For your own notes

Week 26

Czechoslovakia, Hungary and Poland

In the 9th and 10th centuries the coming of Christianity in these areas coincided with the beginning of their national consciousness. In all three countries the people had to struggle to secure national integrity and to preserve their culture through centuries of occupation and division. In each the Roman Catholic Church is in a majority and at the time of the Reformation (whose forerunner in these parts was John Hus) and the Counter-Reformation there were violent struggles for the religious allegiance of the people. All suffered occupation during World War II. Subsequently all three became socialist republics.

The churches in the post-war period, though their situations differed in many respects, faced similar problems in coming to terms with these secularized systems. After the Stalinist period most of them have shown a renewed vitality. The life of the Church is strongly supported by its members with church seminaries and academies training a new generation of priests and pastors.

The Czechoslovak Socialist Republic (1948) is a federal republic consisting of two nations with equal rights (Czechs and Slovaks). In a population of about 15 million some 70% are Roman Catholics, 12% Orthodox and Protestants. There is a small Jewish community of roughly 80,000.

The People's Republic of Hungary (1949), with a population of 10 1/2 million, is an industrial and agrarian nation. In the 16th century a majority of the people became Protestant, but the Counter-Reformation of the next two centuries reversed this situation. Today about 60% of the population is Roman Catholic. Protestants (Reformed 19% and Lutheran 4%), Orthodox and small communities of Baptists, Methodists and Jews, comprise the remaining religious groupings.

The Polish People's Republic (1947) has a population of some 34 million. During the Second World War, over 6 million Polish people, half of them Jewish, were killed. Today a high proportion of the population is under nineteen years of age. Poland is overwhelmingly a Catholic country (estimated at above 93%). The non-Roman Catholic churches — Polish Catholic, Lutheran, Reformed, Methodist, United Evangelical, Orthodox and Mariavite — are all associated in the Polish Ecumenical Council. The Jewish community in Poland, numbering 3 1/4 million prior to the last war, numbers only 7,000 today.

The main problems in each country are the religious education of children and young people, the spread of secularism to the rural areas and the weakness of ecumenical relations between Catholics and Protestants.

A deep concern for the Church's biblical and historical heritage is manifest in the churches, as well as an openness to the questions of daily life and a common emphasis on the proclamation of the Gospel and Christian service in society. Ecumenical cooperation has recently been evident in the new Czech translation of the Bible.

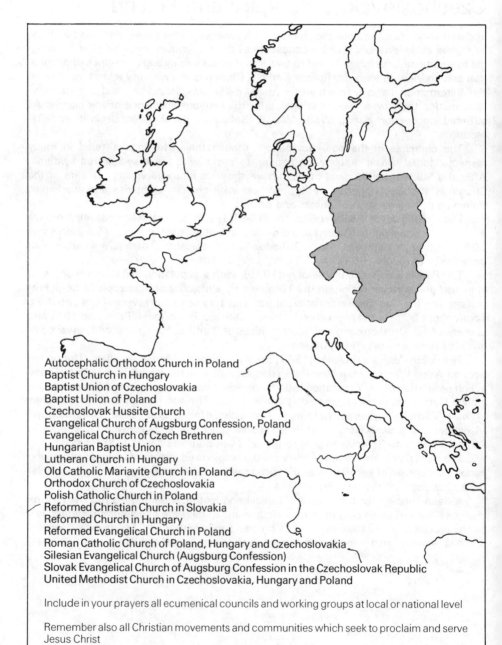

Autocephalic Orthodox Church in Poland
Baptist Church in Hungary
Baptist Union of Czechoslovakia
Baptist Union of Poland
Czechoslovak Hussite Church
Evangelical Church of Augsburg Confession, Poland
Evangelical Church of Czech Brethren
Hungarian Baptist Union
Lutheran Church in Hungary
Old Catholic Mariavite Church in Poland
Orthodox Church of Czechoslovakia
Polish Catholic Church in Poland
Reformed Christian Church in Slovakia
Reformed Church in Hungary
Reformed Evangelical Church in Poland
Roman Catholic Church of Poland, Hungary and Czechoslovakia
Silesian Evangelical Church (Augsburg Confession)
Slovak Evangelical Church of Augsburg Confession in the Czechoslovak Republic
United Methodist Church in Czechoslovakia, Hungary and Poland

Include in your prayers all ecumenical councils and working groups at local or national level

Remember also all Christian movements and communities which seek to proclaim and serve Jesus Christ

For Prayer and Intercession

Give thanks . . .

for the untiring commitment to the Christian faith through long centuries of suffering and persecution of the peoples;
for the vitality of their faith in Christ of these countries in face of a secular ideology and its challenges.

Pray . . .

for the churches in Czechoslovakia, Hungary and Poland, for their pastors and bishops, educators, teachers and social workers and for their parishes and religious communities, that they may be strengthened in their faith and confess Jesus Christ to all people, especially children and young people;
for the churches as they grow in deeper ecumenical fellowship to share their gifts in truth and unity;
that the holocaust may never be forgotten and that the whole Church may find a new respect for the Jewish people.

Prayer . . .

O most merciful Lord Jesus Christ, draw us to you, poor weak things that we are; for where you do not lead we cannot follow. Give us a strong and willing spirit, that our flesh, infirm though it is, may be moved to follow where you direct it. For without you we are unable to do anything, least of all to be willing to die for your sake. Give us a willing spirit, a heart unafraid to believe what is right, a steadfast hope, that we may endure much for your sake and offer up our lives with joy.

Jan Hus

For your own notes

Week 27

Union of Soviet Socialist Republics (1)

The largest church in the *Soviet Union* is the Russian Orthodox Church with roughly 30 million members which came into existence in the 9th century in and around Kiev, its centre for many centuries. Monasticism soon became a powerful force and played a major part in the evangelization of the people of Russia, leaving an abiding mark on them.

In 1589 the Russian Church became a Patriarchate and Moscow its administrative and spiritual centre, the seat of the Patriarch and the Holy Synod. There are 76 bishoprics and about 10,000 priests. The Patriarch also has jurisdiction over Russian Orthodox churches in many other countries.

In the 17th century a split occured in the Russian Orthodox Church resulting in the formation of several movements of "Old Believers". In 1971, the Russian Orthodox Church decided to abolish its ban on their adherents.

The October Revolution of 1917 brought a new situation for both the country and Church. It was difficult for both sides, especially for the Church, to face the new challenges. There were years of much hardship for many believers. As over many centuries, during the Second World War the Church proved its solidarity with the people in their suffering and defence against the enemy which led to a new appreciation of the Church in society. Motivated by Christian values members of the Church today seek to contribute to a more just society and international peace. The liturgy and the personal life are the focal points of the Orthodox witness.

The Christian faith took root among the Armenian people in the 4th century. Outstanding among the founders of the Church was St. Gregory the Illuminator, the "apostle of Armenia". The Armenian people endured great sufferings, especially at the end of the 19th century and from 1914 to 1916, under the Turks. Over 1 million Armenian Christians were massacred. About 3 million live in Soviet Armenia and at least 1 million in other Soviet Republics. There are 35 churches and about 100 priests. The spiritual centre of the whole Armenian Church is Etchmiadzin near Eriwan, the seat of the Catholicos. A great number of Armenians live in diaspora in many countries. They are under the spiritual jurisdiction of the Catholicos.

In Georgia, Christian missionaries were already at work in the 3rd century. Here, too, monasticism played an important role from the start. Around 330, Christianity became the official religion when St. Nino converted the Georgian King Mirian. The church achieved autonomy in 680. Georgian Christians have had an eventful history and experience many trials. Today the Georgian Church numbers about 2 1/2 million. It consists of 15 dioceses and has about 200 parishes and priests. Its spiritual head is the Catholicos-Patriarch in Tbilissi.

Armenian Apostolic Church
Communities of Old Believers
Georgian Orthodox Church
Russian Orthodox Church

Include in your prayers all ecumenical councils and working groups at local or national level

Remember also all Christian movements and communities which seek to proclaim and serve
Jesus Christ

For Prayer and Intercession

Give thanks . . . for the fruits of faithful Orthodox witness among the peoples of the Soviet Union, across many centuries;
for the rich tradition of liturgy and spirituality, continuity in teaching and life, of the whole people of God;
for the example of patience and penitence under the mighty hand of God through trials and sufferings.

Pray . . . for the Orthodox churches of the Soviet Union, their patriarchs, bishops, priests and people that they may hear what the Spirit is saying;
that they may continue to help deepen understanding between themselves and other Christian traditions;
that they may be enabled to see Christ's presence and hear his commandment in the oppressed and persecuted of all lands;
for the victory of the Gospel of Christ among all peoples.

Prayers . . . Blessed art thou, O Christ our God, who didst reveal thy wisdom to simple fishermen, sending upon them from above thy Holy Spirit, and thereby catching the universe as in a net. Glory to thee, O thou who lovest mankind.

Troparian for Pentecost

O Lord, I know not what to ask of thee. Thou alone knowest what are my true needs. Thou lovest me more than I know myself how to love. Help me to see my real needs which are concealed from me. I dare not ask either a cross or consolation. I can only wait on thee. My heart is open to thee. Visit and help me, for thy great mercy's sake. Strike me and heal me, cast me down and raise me up. I worship in silence thy holy will and thine inscrutable ways. I offer myself as a sacrifice to thee. I put all my trust in thee. I have no other desire than to fulfill thy will. Teach me how to pray. Pray thou thyself in me.

Metropolitan Philaret of Moscow

Lord, through the shedding of the blood of your saints, gather in joy all the scattered children of your Church, and all who weep bitterly at the sadness of disunity, you who give grace for our salvation.

Armenian Liturgy

For your own notes

Week 28

Union of Soviet Socialist Republics (2)

Besides the Orthodox churches, there exist several Protestant churches in the *Soviet Union*. The most numerous are the Lutherans and the Baptists.

Lutheran congregations sprang up in Russian cities soon after the Reformation, mainly among foreigners in the provinces bordering the Baltic Sea and Finland, where missionary work dated from the Middle Ages. Lutheran and also Reformed churches were established in Estonia, Latvia and Lithuania, chiefly under German influence paramount until the Second World War. At the Counter-Reformation and under Polish influence, Lithuania became mostly Catholic.

The eventful history of these peoples brought great suffering also to their churches. From 1918 to 1940 many Estonians, Latvians and Lithuanians took refuge abroad, founding churches in exile. Lutheran churches governed by bishops and synods continued, however, to exist in the Soviet Republics of Estonia, Latvia and Lithuania.

When in the 18th and 19th centuries some Czars invited German migrants to Russia, large German colonies were established along the lower course of the Volga river and around the Black Sea. Until the Second World War these German-speaking groups numbered well over 1 million. In 1941 they were deported to the eastern Asiatic regions, especially Siberia and Kazakstan. During the 1960's and 1970's many congregations were reestablished. Renewed efforts to end their isolation and to provide assistance followed the renewal of contacts with them in 1976 through the Lutheran World Federation.

There has been a rapid growth of Baptist congregations in Russia during the past 100 years. Even amid the profound upheavals of recent decades they have demonstrated their missionary dynamic. Most of these communities belong to the Union of Evangelical Christian Baptists. In many places they have been joined by Christians of German extraction and since 1954 by Pentecostal communities. At present they have a membership role of about 60,000 and a community probably exceeding 2 million. A small Reformed Church exists in the Carpatho-Ukraine. Lutherans, Baptists and the Reformed are actively cooperating in international ecumenical organizations.

The relations between Roman Catholicism and Orthodoxy have had a chequered history. There have been attempts to bring Eastern Christians under the jurisdiction of Rome. Today the 3 million plus Roman Catholics in the U.S.S.R. live in Lithuania, the Western Ukraine and areas bordering Poland. Pastoral care and oversight of the churches and training for the priesthood present difficult problems not yet completely solved.

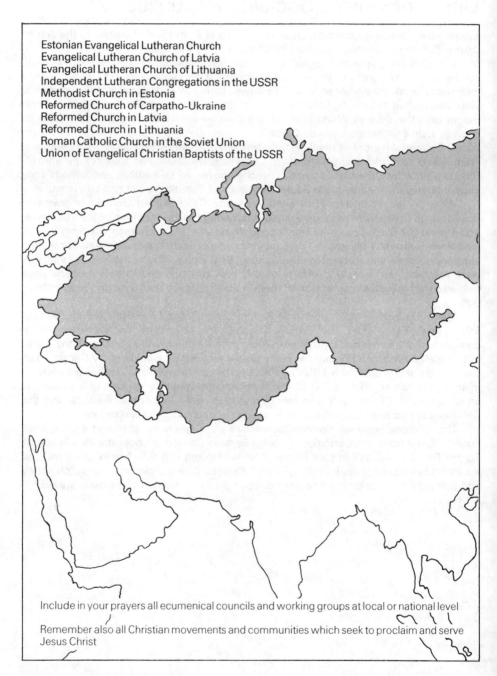

Estonian Evangelical Lutheran Church
Evangelical Lutheran Church of Latvia
Evangelical Lutheran Church of Lithuania
Independent Lutheran Congregations in the USSR
Methodist Church in Estonia
Reformed Church of Carpatho-Ukraine
Reformed Church in Latvia
Reformed Church in Lithuania
Roman Catholic Church in the Soviet Union
Union of Evangelical Christian Baptists of the USSR

Include in your prayers all ecumenical councils and working groups at local or national level

Remember also all Christian movements and communities which seek to proclaim and serve Jesus Christ

For Prayer and Intercession

Give thanks . . . for the minority Christian communities in the countries of the Soviet Union—Baptist, Lutheran, Reformed, Catholic, Pentecostal;
for their witness to the suffering Christ and his presence in the trials and tribulations of his witnesses;
for their evangelical zeal, their love of the Scriptures and service of the freedom of the Gospel.

Pray . . . for all pastors and congregations that they may be upheld and strengthened in their faith, hope and love;
for all those who risk obloquy and penalties for their faith and obedience;
for Christian families—parents and children, old people and young men and women—seeking to follow Christ and to be his witnesses among their fellows and in their community;
for the victory of the Gospel of Christ among all peoples;
for all in authority that they may be led by truth and justice in their efforts for the welfare of all entrusted to their care.

Prayers . . . Eternal God, our Heavenly Father, we intercede for the Church throughout the world, that thou wouldst bless all congregations to whom thou hast entrusted the precious treasure of the Gospel, preserving them in faith and kindling within them the spirit of unity, of generosity, of devotion and missionary zeal, through Jesus Christ our Lord. Amen.

Lord, even before we were born, you had your plan for us. You engaged us to be your witnesses to others. But we are weak and our words are powerless. Put therefore your Word in our mouths and hearts. Help us to go where you send us and to speak what you command. Be beside us Lord, and fill our hearts and minds with your Holy Spirit, that he may glorify you and praise your name in us.
Through Jesus Christ our Lord. Amen.

For your own notes

The People's Republic of China and Hong Kong

Christian history in China began over a thousand years ago as a result of the Nestorian Missions. (The Nestorian Church was divided from the Orthodox after 5th century doctrinal debates.) In the 7th century Jesuit and other Catholic missionary orders preached in China with some success.

The modern missionary impact on China, however, dates from the early 19th century when the Church accompanied the growth of western commercial and political imperialism. By the mid-20th century, Christians numbered about 4 million (with four Roman Catholics to every Protestant), less than 1 % of the population. They were widely distributed across China, with the largest communities located in the coastal provinces. The churches were doing extensive educational and welfare work and could lay claim to the emergence of some Christian political leadership. The churches also played an important role in China's process of modernization.

Following the establishment of the People's Republic in 1949, the churches were reorganized under the guidance of the Bureau of Religious Affairs. All institutional work was given up to the government or the local community. The churches broke their dependency on western financial and personnel support and structural changes took place to meet the demands of the new social order. National organizations were established to help the churches adapt to national goals—the Protestant "Patriotic Three-Self Movement" (called in 1978 the All-China Association of Protestant Churches) and the Roman Catholic "Patriotic Association" (which replaced the old hierarchy). Both Roman Catholic and Protestant membership declined sharply. Overseas contacts were all but completely severed.

In 1967 the Cultural Revolution required the closing of all churches and remaining theological schools. The last formal organizations were dissolved and organized church structures disappeared. Public meetings were temporarily forbidden. There are, however, two or three churches in Peking where Sunday services are held and foreigners are welcomed.

In the last decade Christians (where groups are still extant) have been working out new patterns of life and worship. The number of clergy, few of whom are now full-time church workers, is declining, and Christian groups depend on such natural lay leadership as arises. Worship takes place in whatever locations are convenient and at whatever times. The home is the key to the maintenance of Christian faith and tradition. But reports seem to indicate that it is not only a close but also a self-renewing community, dedicated to faithfulness to the biblical revelation and loyal service to the people. The government policy developed in 1977 renews the recognition of religious communities as legitimate groups in the new society.

The Church in the British Crown Colony of *Hong Kong* has grown in the last generation so that it now numbers about 10 % of the population—some 450,000. Slightly more than 50 % are Roman Catholics, the others being members of the mainstream Protestant groups and numerous independent congregations.

An instrument of educational and welfare work, its presence as a source of comfort, encouragement, community and social reform is strongly evident in Hong Kong. It has close ties with the world Christian community.

The Christian Community in China

Churches in Hong Kong
Anglican Diocese of Hong Kong
Baptist Convention of Hong Kong
Chinese Rhenish Church, Hong Kong Synod
Evangelical Lutheran Church of Hong Kong
Free Methodist Church
Hong Kong Council of the Church of Christ in China
Lutheran Synod, Hong Kong Conference
Methodist Church of Hong Kong
Roman Catholic Diocese
Salvation Army
Tsung Tsin Mission – Hong Kong

Include in your prayers all ecumenical councils and working groups at local or national level

Remember also all Christian movements and communities which seek to proclaim and serve Jesus Christ

For Prayer and Intercession

Give thanks . . .   for the people in China, and their ancient culture with its delicate yet enduring treasures;
for the new hope that has come to millions in China;
for the saints and martyrs who have witnessed to Christ's love in China, and the faithful who persist in a hope founded on the resurrected Lord;
for the life and witness of the Church in Hong Kong.

Pray . . .   for the Church in China, that it may have wisdom to discover new and creative forms of life in the People's Republic, the commitment to serve in building the nation, the courage to witness to the Gospel in the presence of danger, the love to overcome suspicion and fear, and the patience to wait and hope in the Lord;
for the continued vitality of the Church in Hong Kong, and the strengthening of its reconciling and loving ministries among the people.

Prayers . . .   O Lord, who likened your disciples to salt and to leaven, give to your faithful in China, scattered and few as they are, the power of your Spirit, that in their integrity, selflessness and love they may be examples to their neighbours and testify to your Glory.   Amen.

O God, increase and strengthen the unity of spirit which has been nurtured in the total Christian fellowship of Hong Kong. Sustain this spirit of Christian Unity that it may take deeper root in all communions. Through growing trust, may the gifts of the churches be committed to the service of those in spiritual and physical need. And in this service may your kingdom be manifest among men.
Hong Kong Christian Council

For your own notes

Japan, Korea and Taiwan

Japan made its first link with Christianity in 1549 when Francis Xavier landed in Kagoshima, Southern Japan. Mass conversions took place, followed by suppression and persecution of Christian converts by the government. In 1859 the first Protestant missionaries from the Episcopal Church in the USA entered Japan. For more than a century the witness of the Protestant and Roman Catholic churches has made a considerable impact on this island nation deeply influenced by Buddhism, Confucianism and Shintoism.

During the Second World War, government pressure, added to the latent desire for Protestant unity, led to the formation of the Nihon Krisuto Kyodan (The United Church of Christ in Japan) in which over 30 denominations came together. The Kyodan has remained a major Christian body, despite some internal tensions. It continues to witness to Christ together with other Protestant churches, the Roman Catholic Church and the Orthodox Church, the latter stemming from Russian Orthodox influence in the 19th century.

Japan has a population of 112 million of which about 1 % professes the Christian faith. In a country where industrialization presents new challenges and new religions such as Soka Gakkai co-exist with religions of long tradition, it becomes even more important to witness as a united Church.

Christian work began in *Korea* in 1784 when the Korean, Sung-Hoo Lee, baptized by Jesuits in Peking, returned home. Protestant missionaries followed towards the end of the 19th century. Besides proclaiming the Gospel, the churches did pioneering work in education, medicine and social work. More recently, they have demonstrated strong vitality in their witness in difficult social and political situations and in numerical growth. Five percent of the total population of about 35 million is Christian.

The churches in Korea are churches of martyrs. Imbued with the love of God, they witnessed to Jesus Christ under Japanese colonial rule (1910-1945). The Korean War was another severe test of faith for Korean Christians. Those in South Korea continue to bear the torch of conscience before the entire nation in the present politically adverse situation. Little is known of the situation of Christians in North Korea.

Taiwan first came into contact with Christianity through 17th-century Dutch traders in Asia. In 1859 Dominican priests arrived from South China with the resulting strong Roman Catholic presence of today. They were followed by Presbyterian missionaries from Britain in 1865 and from Canada in 1872. Christians today are about 5 % of the 16.7 million population. After the establishment of the People's Republic of China in 1949, many other Protestant denominations moved across the Taiwan Strait to Taiwan.

Churches in Taiwan have concentrated on evangelism, education and medical service. Taiwan's uncertain political future and the tensions between different groups have made Christians acutely aware of their responsibility to society. Some have called for self-determination as the way to settle its political future.

Anglican Church in Japan, Korea and Taiwan
Chinese Baptist Convention
Church of Christ in Japan
Free Methodist Church – Republic of China
Free Methodist Church in Japan
Japan Evangelical Lutheran Church
Japan Lutheran Church
Japan Baptist Convention – Japan Baptist Union
Japanese Orthodox Church
Kinki Evangelical Lutheran Church
Korea Baptist Convention
Korean Christian Church in Japan
Korean Methodist Church
Lutheran Church in Korea and Taiwan
Methodist Church in Korea
Methodist Church of the Republic of China
Presbyterian Church in Korea and Taiwan
Presbyterian Church in the Republic of Korea
Roman Catholic Church – Japan, Korea and Taiwan
Salvation Army – Japan, Korea and Taiwan
Taiwan Lutheran Church
United Church of Christ in Japan
West Japan Evangelical Lutheran Church

Include in your prayers all ecumenical councils and working groups at local or national level

Remember also all Christian movements and communities which seek to proclaim and serve Jesus Christ

For Prayer and Intercession

Give thanks . . .   for the Church and continuing Christian witness in the midst of many faiths and ideologies;
for the courageous faith of those who have been striving for a more human life for all, often at great risk to themselves.

Pray . . .   that the churches might find unity and the Gospel may spread in Japan, Korea and Taiwan;
for those who are oppressed that they might have freedom;
for those who are discriminated against that their human rights might be respected;
for those who are isolated and separated that they might find unity and solidarity;
for renewed strength and courage to witness to Christ amidst political uncertainties.

Prayer . . .   O God of Abraham, Isaac, and Jacob, we beseech thee to hear the prayers of thy children whose ancestors knew thee not in this life. Thou knowest them all. Consecrate the bond of kinship which binds us to them, and mercifully make us all partakers in him who died on the cross for the sins of the whole world, who preached to the spirits in prison, and rose again to be ruler over all thy creation, thy Son, our Saviour, Jesus Christ. To him, with thee and the Holy Spirit, be all praise and all glory, for ever and ever, world without end.

Daisuke Kitagawa

For your own notes

Vietnam, Laos, Kampuchea and Thailand

Vietnam, the *Lao People's Democratic Republic* and *Democratic Kampuchea* were colonized by the French, though their complicated history and patterns of relationship reach back many centuries. The French left Vietnam in 1954 then heavy American involvement in the Indochina war caused intense suffering over many years.

All three countries, predominantly Buddhist, have relatively small Christian communities. The main church is the Roman Catholic. In a population of nearly 41 million, Vietnam has a Catholic community of some 2 million, with one Archbishop in Ho Chi Minh City (formerly Saigon) and another in Hanoi. In the Lao People's Democratic Republic (population nearly 7 million) the Catholics have been recruited from ethnic minorities and in Democratic Kampuchea from the Vietnamese, now largely dispersed.

Protestant work is recent. The American Christian and Missionary Alliance began work in Laos and Vietnam around 1925. This has resulted in a small Evangelical Church of some 5,000 members in Laos and 125,000 in Vietnam. In addition, in Laos and Kampuchea (population over 6 1/2 million) there are small Protestant churches stemming from the work of Swiss and French groups.

In these three countries successive wars in Indochina have had a profound effect on the churches and people, including the conflict in the 1970's between Vietnam and Kampuchea. It is not clear what has become of the Church in Kampuchea, where due to its immense political upheavals there has been little outside communication. In Laos the Roman Catholic Church probably remains intact, but many members of the Evangelical Church have fled across the border into Thailand and beyond.

In 1954, when Vietnam was divided through war, many thousands of Roman Catholics moved south. Their influence on the church contributed to its strong opposition to the changes being fought over. Because it was smaller, the Evangelical Church was less vocal, but shared the same approach. In the north of Vietnam the Roman Catholic and Evangelical churches adapted themselves to life in a new society, their heads being members of the National Assembly. Now that all Vietnam is under one government, the churches of the south are working out new patterns, going through a difficult time of reappraisal and adjustment. There is evidence, however, of a desire on the side of both government and Church to avoid confrontation.

Aware of the present difficulties, the Archbishop of Ho Chi Minh City has called for a dialogue with the Marxists. Recently the Evangelical Church in Laos joined the Christian Conference of Asia (CCA), and there have also been contacts, though more tentative, between the Evangelical Church in Vietnam and the CCA.

In *Thailand* (population 37 million) the Roman Catholic Church is small, its members coming mainly from ethnic minorities. The Church of Christ in Thailand is the result of joint missionary work by the United Presbyterian Church in the USA, the Disciples of Christ and the American Baptists (Northern Convention).

Small in comparison to the population, it has a life and vigour of its own. Relations with the large Buddhist community have been slow in growing, but a Buddhist/Christian joint action for human rights has developed. There are working relationships with Buddhist priests in the rural areas as the Church has become involved in community development programmes.

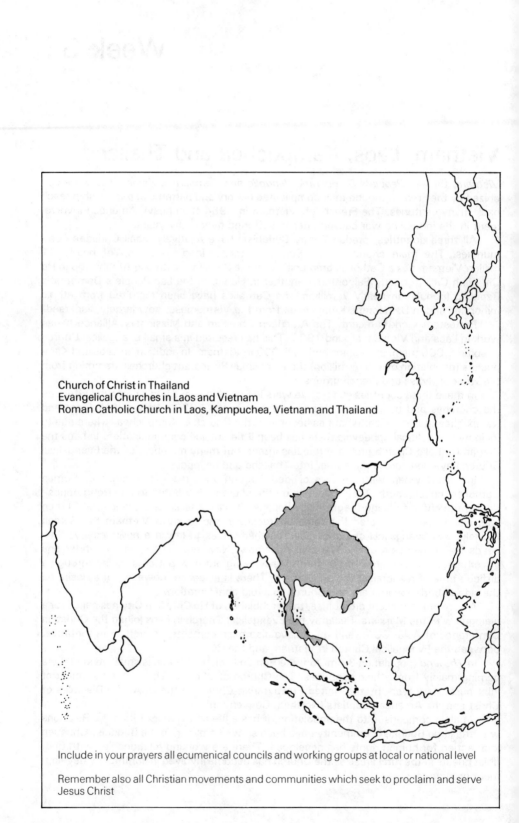

Church of Christ in Thailand
Evangelical Churches in Laos and Vietnam
Roman Catholic Church in Laos, Kampuchea, Vietnam and Thailand

Include in your prayers all ecumenical councils and working groups at local or national level

Remember also all Christian movements and communities which seek to proclaim and serve Jesus Christ

For Prayer and Intercession

Give thanks . . .
that the people of Vietnam, after long years of war, have found national unity;
for the witness of small groups of Christians in Thailand and Laos.

Pray . . .
that the peoples of Vietnam, Laos and Kampuchea may be granted freedom and peaceful development to live their life as independent nations;
that the wounds of the successive wars may be healed;
that throughout the region families may be settled again and all uprooted people find a place to live and work to sustain them;
that the churches in Thailand may join together to work with their neighbours of other faiths for the benefit of all.

Prayer . . .
Lord God most high, may we offer thee praise and thankfulness for thy loving kindness in letting us hear about thy precious Gospel. We are happy to be called Christians, and so make us all real ones. Grant us the power to feel thy presence among us. Cleanse our hearts and make them clear like crystals in order that we may see thee and that the Holy Spirit may dwell in us. Dear Lord . . . there are many friends of ours who have not heard about thy precious name nor have they seen thy light. Help us all to dedicate ourselves more in thy service and to shine for thee. Forgive us for being selfish and letting thy light grow dim. We ask these things in the name of the Great Lord Jesus Christ whose merits lift us from sin.

Prayer of Thai woman

For your own notes

Week 32

Bangladesh, Burma, Nepal and Bhutan

Bangladesh was born in travail, after this former eastern province of Pakistan demanded full autonomy from its western region a thousand miles away, which led to armed action by the central government, civil strife between factions within the province and finally full scale war between India and Pakistan. The new state underwent further conflict after its first president was assassinated.

With 75 million people, mostly dependent on agriculture, living in 141,000 square miles, Bangladesh is extremely poor. Its Christians are 1% of the population—mainly Roman Catholics and adherents of the Baptist, Anglican and Lutheran traditions. The National Council of Churches includes 10 churches with other organizations as associates. It has several coordinating committees. The Christian Commission for Development is one, handling relief and development, which takes priority in the present situation stemming from war damage and severe economic problems.

Burma, freed from British rule in 1948, is ruled by the Revolutionary Council which leads the Burma Socialist Programme Party, the only party in the country. There is freedom of religion: 84% are Buddhist. Christians number about 950,000, 3% of the total population. The majority are Baptists; about 1/3 Roman Catholics. Methodists and Anglicans and several sects are also present.

Gradually the government has taken over all private institutions, including Christian and Buddhist schools. Residence permits for foreigners are only renewed if applicants are needed for the country's development. Travel abroad for private delegations or individuals is discouraged.

Though a rice-rich country with oil and other mineral resources, economic development has been slow, affected by political and tribal problems. Changes in the country have pushed the churches into self-reliance. There have been several thousand converts yearly. There is need to equip the laity spiritually for whatever the future might bring. Contacts and opportunities for fellowship with Christians abroad would be welcomed.

Nepal is a small, mountainous country in the high Himalayas to the north of India. The people are deeply religious Hindus. Many move constantly in and out of India for trade and employment. The population of 11 million, mainly agricultural and largely illiterate, is ruled by hereditary kings. Some have paid attention to education and economic development. Traditional missionary work is not allowed; conversion is an offence. There have been contacts with Christians across the border for many years and now there are a few congregations in a national fellowship with an annual conference. It sponsors evangelism and Bible schools.

The churches are self-supporting. The first full Bible in Nepali has been published recently. There are nearly 200 missionaries related to the United Mission in Nepal which has an agreement with the government running hospitals, schools and development projects, and 30 members of Catholic teaching orders in Nepal.

Next to Nepal are *Bhutan* (1 million population), an independent Buddhist state since 1971, with a history of British and Indian links, and the smallest of the Himalayan kingdoms *Sikkim*, mainly Buddhist. It seeks from India the same form of independence as Bhutan. All main religions are present—there is a Church of Scotland and Scandinavian Alliance Mission.

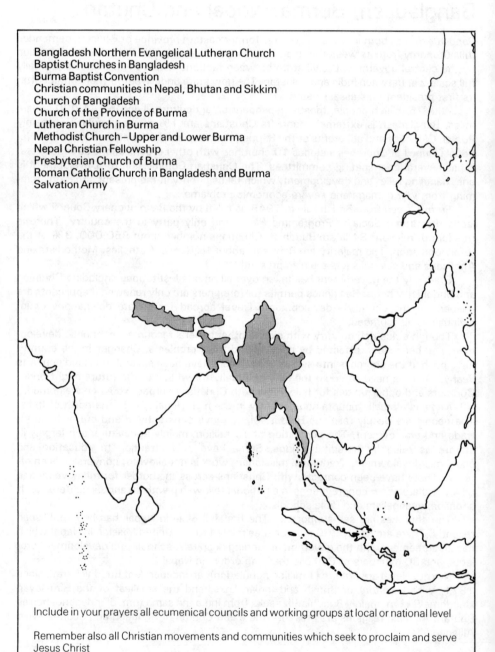

Bangladesh Northern Evangelical Lutheran Church
Baptist Churches in Bangladesh
Burma Baptist Convention
Christian communities in Nepal, Bhutan and Sikkim
Church of Bangladesh
Church of the Province of Burma
Lutheran Church in Burma
Methodist Church – Upper and Lower Burma
Nepal Christian Fellowship
Presbyterian Church of Burma
Roman Catholic Church in Bangladesh and Burma
Salvation Army

Include in your prayers all ecumenical councils and working groups at local or national level

Remember also all Christian movements and communities which seek to proclaim and serve Jesus Christ

For Prayer and Intercession

Give thanks . . .   for the courage and zeal with which Christians are living their faith in the midst of serious political troubles and natural disasters;
for the commitment of churches and related groups to foster development and self-reliance.

Pray . . .   for the unity of the churches in Bangladesh, that their cooperation in the National Council of Churches may grow and flourish in a committed fellowship with a common witness;
for the enormous task of rehabilitation and development in Bangladesh, for a stable political structure and a just society, and for friendly relations with the large neighbouring countries of India, Burma and China;
for unity among the churches in Burma that they may draw closer together and strengthen their self-reliance in the Christian fellowship;
for greater opportunities for the Christians in Burma to be together with Christians of other countries;
that Christians of Nepal may be given wisdom to see their mission in a situation where this is prescribed.

Prayers . . .   O Saviour Christ, in whose way of love lies the secret of all life, and the hope of all men, we pray for quiet courage to match this hour. We did not choose to be born or to live in such an age; but let its problems challenge us, its discoveries exhilarate us, its injustices anger us, its possibilities inspire us, and its vigour renew us, for your kingdom's sake.

O God, we thank you for the glorious opportunities
   to build new societies
   of peace, justice and love
   to praise and glorify you.
Help us, we pray,
      to stand up with courage,
      to work with love
      and to live in hope
For Christ's sake.

For your own notes

The Invisible Community of the Suffering

The Church of God would be incomplete without the invisible community of the suffering—invisible not only for its lack of a body, a structured organization, but also invisible because many of the sufferings cannot be seen by the eye.

It is a harsh reality that we human beings inflict such great suffering upon one another. People brought Jesus to the cross, and people continue to crucify their brothers and sisters every day. The occasions are manifold: from the victims of an air-crash to the terrors of war; from imprisonment in isolation cells to anonymous death in the overcrowded streets of large cities of Asia and Europe; from undernourished children in Africa to those left without human care in the Americas. We are just beginning to suspect the sufferings which will result from our careless pollution of the earth and space around us and to fear the pain of genetic damage which could result from unrestricted experimentation. The more we are able to "make" things, the more we become the cause of evil and suffering.

Even more suffering is caused by forces beyond our control: earthquakes, and volcanic eruptions, diseases and many forms of mental and physical handicap.

When we contemplate the enormity of human suffering, we are driven to ask "Why?" Why must people suffer? Why must I suffer? . . . the old but ageless question of Job . . .

There is no answer. Job did not receive an answer. The only response was the revelation of God himself. He spoke to Job. Today God reveals himself to us in Jesus Christ, the Suffering Servant, who died in agony on a cross. In his passion, he gave a mysterious quality to all suffering, and through his suffering, he calls all who suffer to share in an invisible community made holy by his special love for them.

It would be preposterous for the Church to glorify suffering. Christ himself, in a curiously ironic way, calls his followers equally to bear his cross and to lift it from others. His days on this earth were spent in deeds of compassion, and he calls us to a ministry that gives a priority to the needs of the hungry, the thirsty, the homeless, and the imprisoned. To ignore the plight of the suffering would be blasphemy against God, who will judge us all with these words:

> "Truly, I say to you, as you did it to one of
> the least of these my brethren, you did it to me."

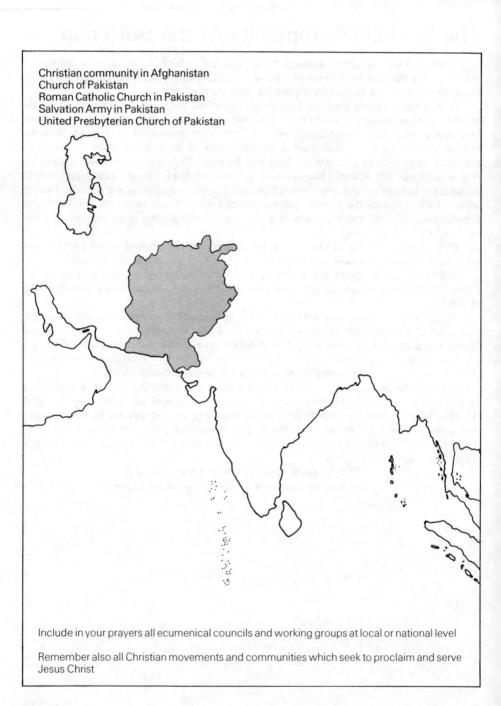

Christian community in Afghanistan
Church of Pakistan
Roman Catholic Church in Pakistan
Salvation Army in Pakistan
United Presbyterian Church of Pakistan

Include in your prayers all ecumenical councils and working groups at local or national level

Remember also all Christian movements and communities which seek to proclaim and serve Jesus Christ

For Prayer and Intercession

Give thanks . . .   for the revelation of God who comes to us in suffering and hallows each moment that we offer to him;
for the promise of the Comforter who comes to sustain us and to share our burdens;
for the ministries of persons who come in Christ's name to those who suffer, bringing the gifts and skills to make life better;
for those who struggle to establish peace and justice and who press for the realization of human rights.

Pray . . .   for those who suffer pain;
for those who suffer mental and emotional distress;
for those who are physically handicapped;
for those whose minds cannot develop;
for those who are victims of oppression, war and injustice;
for those who are starving;
for those who suffer alone;
for those who suffer through sharing the pains of those whom they love;
for those who know that they will soon die;
for those who cannot wait to die.

Prayer . . .   Almighty God, who hast shown us in the life and teaching of thy Son the true way of blessedness, thou hast also shown us in his suffering and death that the path of love may lead to a cross, and the reward of faithfulness may be a crown of thorns. Give us grace to learn these hard lessons.
May we take up our cross and follow Christ in the strength of patience and the constancy of faith; and may we have such fellowship with him in his sorrow that we may know the secret of his strength and peace, and see even in our darkest hour the shining of the eternal light; for his sake who died and rose again for us, the same Jesus Christ our Lord.

John Hunter

For your own notes

Pakistan and Afghanistan

Pakistan came into existence when British rule ended on the Indian sub-continent in 1947. The predominantly Muslim areas in the west and east became a separate state, with over a thousand miles of Indian territory in between. The eastern province broke away in 1971 to become Bangladesh. When Pakistan's founder died, there was a period of political strife, then military rule, with armed conflicts with India. The upheavals in the east led to another war with India. Following that, the country had a period of civilian government; relations with India improved and steps towards a return to democracy taken, including a general election. However, in 1977, the country came again under military rule.

Over 93% of the 63 million population is Muslim; Islamic culture is predominant. Some political leaders still favour the Islamic way of life for the country, though efforts are maintained to secure full rights for religious minorities, including participation in political parties. Christians number about two million (about 3% of the population).

Like other developing countries, Pakistan has a low per capita income. Planned development has been attempted, though many resources have been needed for defence. Economic prospects have brightened with government emphasis on agrarian reform and the discovery of high grade oil.

The history of the churches in Pakistan is part of the history of Christianity in the northern part of the sub-continent, beginning with the work of several Christian missions from the 16th century onwards. The Church of Pakistan is the result of a union of churches of Anglican, Lutheran, Methodist and Church of Scotland traditions; its membership accounts for one third of the Christians. The United Presbyterian Church did not join. Half the Christians are Roman Catholic (many from Goa), coordinated by the Catholic Bishop's Conference which cooperates with the National Council of churches, with which the Protestant churches are affiliated.

Christians in Pakistan, including their scholars, teachers, social workers and lawyers, are appreciated highly for their contributions, but face the usual problems of identity and participation in the social and political life of a small religious minority, including subtle discrimination in employment. There is no legal bar to evangelistic work, but the propagation of the Gospel is not always welcomed.

On the whole Christians are poor. In rural areas most are landless labourers. The churches are striving to develop leadership and employment potential through education and self-help projects.

Afghanistan is an orthodox Muslim state of 20 million, landlocked between Pakistan, the Soviet Union and Iran. The only Christian presence in the country is the group of people working in government service from other countries and members of foreign and diplomatic communities living there.

For Prayer and Intercession

Give thanks . . .   for the witness of Christians in Pakistan, their courage and commitment in the midst of a predominantly Muslim population.

Pray . . .   that the tiny minority of Christians may be strengthened in their faith and witness;
that religious freedom may be safeguarded;
that political stability may be found, harmony between all people maintained and economic development and educational improvement be secured for all citizens;
that all churches may be fully united and a common witness to Christ be made possible.

Prayer . . .   Blessed be thou, Almighty Father of our Lord Jesus Christ, for thy guiding power which has brought us here to serve thee in this church. Look upon us, we beseech thee, who are called by the name of thy dear Son, and grant that we may ever walk worthily of our Christian vocation. Unite us all in mutual love and forbearance; put far from us all selfish indifference to the needs of others; and give us grace gladly to bear our burdens and fulfil our duties as members of this church and citizens of this country, to the glory of thy name; through the same Jesus Christ, our Lord.   Amen.
From the inauguration services of the Church of Pakistan

For your own notes

Week 35

India

India is a land of 600 million people of different languages and ethnic groups, living on a sub-continent with widely varying terrain and climate. About 85 % of the people are Hindus and 8 % Muslims. Christians form the third largest community with about 15 million adherents, or 2.5 % of the total, followed by Sikhs, Buddhists and others. Over half the Christians are Roman Catholic.

India was led to freedom from British rule in 1947 by Mahatma Gandhi and other illustrious leaders who laid the foundations for building a liberal socialist democracy with a parliamentary system of government. The Congress Party was in power till the mid-1970's. Since then, the Central Government has been led by a coalition headed by the Janata Party.

Though there has been some progress, the country still faces immense problems of building a national community from many religions, cultures and languages, of solving the massive poverty and unemployment, and of developing people's participation in economic development and social transformation within a political democracy.

The origins of Christianity in India are traced to the 4th century and traditionally to the coming of St. Thomas the Apostle in the first century as claimed by the Syrian Christians. The Roman Catholic hierarchy goes back to 1558. Protestant churches grew up from the work of numerous missionary societies from the West.

Because of this varied history, Christians today are unevenly distributed, 75 % in South India, 15 % in tribal areas in North-East India. Others are thinly spread across North India.

Efforts to end the many confessional divisions began early in the 20th century, aided by ecumenical youth movements like the YMCA, the YWCA and the SCM and the launching of the Christian Council of India, now called the Council of Churches in India. Close collaboration between Roman Catholics, Orthodox and Protestants has grown at all levels, including conversations on faith and order matters and the creation of ecumenical ashrams.

The Church of South India (1947) and the Church of North India (1970) are landmarks in ecumenical history. Many Christians in India, of the Baptist, Lutheran, United Methodist, Orthodox and Syrian traditions are still separate. Conversations are going on between the CSI, the CNI and the Mar Thoma churches, and the CSI and the Lutherans in South India for wider union.

Parallel with this movement towards unity, churches in India increasingly have been taking over responsibility for mission and sending and supporting Indian workers in other Asian countries.

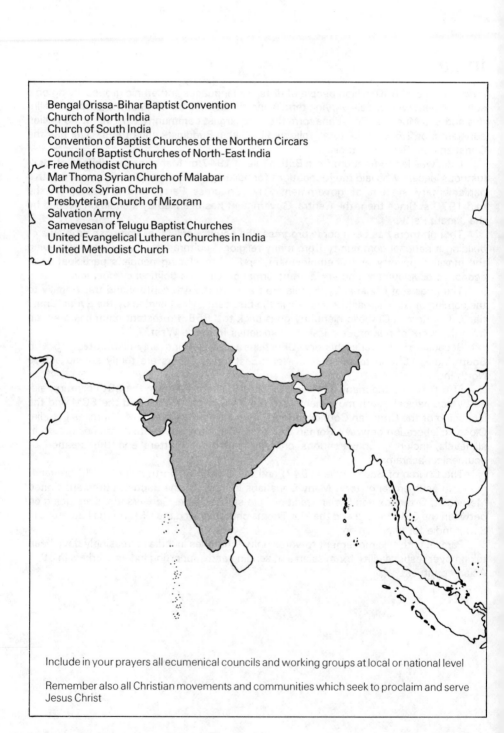

Bengal Orissa-Bihar Baptist Convention
Church of North India
Church of South India
Convention of Baptist Churches of the Northern Circars
Council of Baptist Churches of North-East India
Free Methodist Church
Mar Thoma Syrian Church of Malabar
Orthodox Syrian Church
Presbyterian Church of Mizoram
Salvation Army
Samevesan of Telugu Baptist Churches
United Evangelical Lutheran Churches in India
United Methodist Church

Include in your prayers all ecumenical councils and working groups at local or national level

Remember also all Christian movements and communities which seek to proclaim and serve Jesus Christ

For Prayer and Intercession

Give thanks . . .
for the many centuries of faithful witness by the churches of India, and for their missionary outreach today;
for the pioneering role of these churches and outstanding leaders within the wider ecumenical movement, the steps they have taken towards unity and reconciliation, and their broadening quest for the full unity that is Christ's will for his Church;
for the involvement of Christians in building bridges of understanding with people of other faiths and their contribution to nation-building.

Pray . . .
that the churches may see more clearly and embody more courageously the unity in faith and witness to which they are called;
that they may be cleansed of prejudices of caste, sex and language, and strengthened in their testimony to the healing power of Christ;
that the Church in India may be a sign of hope for the despairing, of faith for those who search, and of love for those whose love has grown cold.

Prayer . . .
Our Father, we pray that the Church may be one in Christ, a true fellowship of the cloud of witnesses and of all those who now love and serve our Lord Jesus Christ. May the churches be conscious of their oneness in thee and speak the word of healing to this troubled world. For the sake of Jesus Christ.

Sarah Chakko

For your own notes

Week 36

Sri Lanka and Islands of the Indian Ocean

The churches in *Sri Lanka* date from its colonial occupation. The first were the Roman Catholics during the Portuguese regime in the 16th and 17th centuries. The Dutch Reformed Church followed in the 17th century. Other Protestant churches were founded during the British period, from the early 19th century onwards.

Sri Lanka has about 13 million people, 71 % of them Sinhalese. The remainder are Ceylon and Indian Tamils, Moors, Burghers and Europeans, some Malays and others.

The majority of the population (65 %) follow Buddhism, introduced from India in 247 BC. Next is Hinduism (18 %), with Christians forming 9 % and Muslims 8 %. There is complete religious freedom in the country. All religions are dealt with by the government on an equal footing (with regard to religious broadcasting for example). Religion is compulsory in schools. Children are taught their religion by a teacher of their faith. The main festivals are national holidays. There are no official restraints on publishing religious material, or on religious activity in general.

On matters of national interest the churches frequently act in consultation. Much still remains to be done, however, to foster ecumenical activity in congregations. The Anglican, Methodist, Presbyterian and Baptist churches in Sri Lanka, together with the Church of South India which has one diocese in the country, have been engaged in negotiations for church union, and "The Scheme of Church Union in Sri Lanka" was voted on and accepted as the basis for forming "The Church of Sri Lanka". Implementation of the union, however, was prevented by court action by those opposed to it. While necessary legal steps are being taken over this, the churches continue their various ecumenical programmes of worship, study and action, and consultations on union continue.

The Study Centre for Religion and Society in Colombo runs a programme of inter-religious dialogue for Protestants, Buddhists and Roman Catholics. The journal *Dialogue* is published by the Centre with editorial collaboration from the other groups. Much common search has been shared. One of the immediate tasks is to find a mutually acceptable theological basis for a pluralistic society in the future.

In the Indian Ocean, off the Indian sub-continent, are the *Maldives*, over 1,000 islands, linked in an independent Republic since 1968. The mixed descent population of South Indians, Sinhalese, Arabs are Sunni Muslims. The (Anglican) Church of the Province of the Indian Ocean has dioceses in Mauritius, Madagascar, the Seychelles and elsewhere in the region.

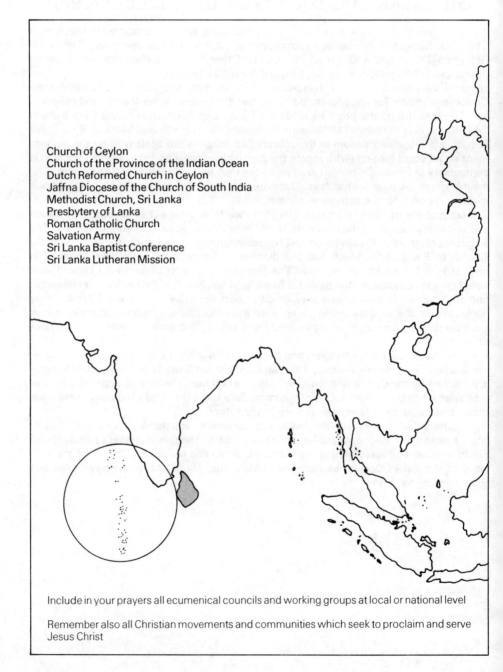

Church of Ceylon
Church of the Province of the Indian Ocean
Dutch Reformed Church in Ceylon
Jaffna Diocese of the Church of South India
Methodist Church, Sri Lanka
Presbytery of Lanka
Roman Catholic Church
Salvation Army
Sri Lanka Baptist Conference
Sri Lanka Lutheran Mission

Include in your prayers all ecumenical councils and working groups at local or national level

Remember also all Christian movements and communities which seek to proclaim and serve Jesus Christ

For Prayer and Intercession

Give thanks . . .

for the life and witness of Christians in Sri Lanka;
for the constitutional rights freely to proclaim the Gospel of Jesus Christ and to educate young people in his ways;
for the search for unity in which many Christians are actively engaged.

Pray . . .

for peace and friendly relations between the two major ethnic groups, Sinhala and Tamil, and for harmony among all people in Sri Lanka;
for the restructuring of the society and economy of the country to eliminate poverty and the disparities of wealth and privilege;
for large numbers of young people who, after receiving an education, are unable to find employment or to make a livelihood for themselves;
for the overcoming of all hindrances and the speedy consummation of union among the churches;
for Christians of the islands of the Indian Ocean, that across great distances and in the midst of ethnic diversity they may know the unity that is Christ's gift.

Prayer . . .

O God, the Parent of our Lord Jesus Christ, and our Parent: thou who art to us both Father and Mother: We who are thy children draw around thy lotus feet to worship thee. Thy compassion is as the fragrance of the lotus. Though thou art enthroned in the heavens, we may draw nigh to thee; for thy feet stand upon the earth where we humans dwell. Thy Son, our Lord, was man.

We see thy compassion in Jesus. He gives content to the Hindu name for thee—Siva, the Kindly One. He gives significance to the Muslim address of thee—Allah, the Merciful. He embodies in the Godhead what the Buddhist worship in the Buddha—compassion itself.

Thou God of all the world, let our history teach us that we belong to thee alone and that thou alone dost belong to us. And thou art enough, for in thee we sinners find sonship and daughterhood again—the one thing that we most need.

D. T. Niles

For your own notes

The Philippines, Malaysia and Singapore

Seven thousand islands make up the *Philippines*; 89% of the 42 million people are Roman Catholic, 3% Protestant. On some southern islands Islam has been the religion since the 14th century. With 16th-century Spanish colonialism, political and ecclesiastical domination went together. Bible reading in local languages was discouraged but in the late 19th century the Scriptures became available through the work of a Dominican missionary.

In 1898 the USA, involved in war with Spain, helped the Philippine revolutionary movement, but the country fell under US (then Japanese 1942-1945) rule. Independence was gained in 1946.

Protestant missions became active and in 1901 many of them, with the YMCA and two Bible societies, formed the Evangelical Union to avoid duplication and help educational, pastoral, medical and agricultural work.

In 1902, the indigenous Filipino Independent Church was formed by some Roman Catholics, followed later by the Iglesia Evangélica Metodista and the Iglesia Ni Christo, the fastest growing religious group. These churches made a major contribution to indigenization and self-determination. Union Theological Seminary, founded in Manila in 1907, has trained generations of church leaders.

In 1948 some Protestant denominations united, together with indigenous groups, to form the United Church of Christ. A National Council of Churches was created in 1963.

Roman Catholics and Protestants joined together in 1970 to form the Philippine Ecumenical Council on Community Organization to help deprived groups develop their awareness. One organization they helped create received the Pope's blessing during his visit.

The churches have worked together on issues of land reform, people imprisoned for their views, problems of poverty and wealth between rulers and ruled in a situation where martial law was declared in 1972.

The 12 million inhabitants of *Malaysia* (East and West) represent Malay, Chinese, Indian, Eurasian and European groups. Much of the country is still jungle, inhabited by the original tribes, their faith predominantly Muslim. The Chinese religion is an amalgam of animism, Mahayana Buddhism and Confucianism. Malaysia was dominated in turn by Portuguese, Dutch and British settlers. The British missionary societies spread the Christian faith and opened schools, though the British government prevented mission work among the Malay Muslims. Today Roman Catholic, Syrian, Anglican and many Protestant churches are steadily growing. The churches' work is coordinated through the Council of Churches of Malaysia.

Singapore is an island republic of many ethnic groups (80% are Chinese). There are four main religions. Among the Christians the Methodists are the strongest, then the Anglicans. There is a National Council of Churches. Trinity Theological College is a union body. Fresh church union negotiations were begun in 1967. The many linguistic, cultural and ethnic differences among the Christians are constant challenges to them in ecumenical endeavours.

Anglican Church in Malaysia and Singapore
Basel Christian Church of Malaysia
Convention of Philippine Baptist Churches
Evangelical Lutheran Church in Malaysia and Singapore
Evangelical Methodist Church in the Philippines
Free Methodist Church – Philippines
Lutheran Church in Malaysia and Singapore
Lutheran Church in the Philippines
Malayan Synod of the Chinese Christian Church
Malaysia Baptist Convention
Mar Thoma Syrian Church in Malaysia
Methodist Church in Malaysia
Methodist Church in Singapore
Philippine Independent Church
Presbyterian Church in Malaysia
Presbyterian Church in Singapore
Protestant Church in Sabah
Roman Catholic Church in Philippines, Malaysia and Singapore
Salvation Army
Singapore Baptist Convention
Syrian Orthodox Church in Malaya
United Church of Christ in the Philippines
United Methodist Church – Philippines Central Conference

Include in your prayers all ecumenical councils and working groups at local or national level

Remember also all Christian movements and communities which seek to proclaim and serve Jesus Christ

For Prayer and Intercession

Give thanks . . .
: for Christian witness in the midst of other religions and ideologies;
for the unity and cooperation between churches achieved despite many different languages, cultures and races.

Pray . . .
: for guidance and courage for Christians as they develop their interest in their nation's affairs;
for wisdom and strength, particularly for the people of the Philippines, and the churches there, as they struggle with critical problems and choices towards justice, harmony and prosperity as a nation;
for all Christians in the area in their efforts towards greater ecumenical cooperation and church union.

Prayers . . .
: Lord, make us realize that our Christianity is like a rice field, that when it is newly planted, the paddies are prominent; but as the plants take root and grow taller, these dividing paddies gradually vanish, and soon there appears only one vast continuous field. So give us roots of love and make us grow in Christian fellowship and service, so that thy will be done in our lives, through our Saviour, thy Son, Jesus Christ.

Prayer of Filipino

Lord, in these times when we are about to lose hope and our efforts seem futile, grant that we may perceive in our hearts and minds the image of your resurrection which remains our only source of courage and strength, so that we may continue to face the challenges, and struggle against hardship and oppression born of injustice.

From a liturgy created for use by the people of one of the poorest slum areas of Manila.

For your own notes

Indonesia

Indonesia, the fifth largest nation on earth with 130 million people, is a great archipelago of over 13,000 islands, 6,000 of them inhabited. Eighty-five percent live in rural areas. The main religion is Islam (80%). Christians are 8%, a quarter Roman Catholics. Hindus and Buddhists are about 7%, the remainder are of animistic and other religions.

The earliest immigrants were Malays and Hindus from India, then Chinese, Arabs, Portuguese and finally the Dutch, who colonized and ruled from the early 17th century to 1945. Twentieth-century nationalist movements, becoming strong and unified during World War II, and the Japanese occupation, led the country to independence. Indonesia has a constitution based on *Pancasila* (5 principles) — belief in God, humanism, nationalism, democracy and social justice.

Christianity begins with the Portuguese arrival in the Moluccas and Celebes (1522). With the arrival of the Dutch (1596) Catholic missions disappeared except at Flores and Timor and Protestant churches came into existence, growing through American and European missionary activity, especially in North Sumatra and Java. There was spontaneous growth on Bali island where the Dutch forbade missions.

In 1930 the Batak Church gained autonomy; others soon followed. The churches became self-reliant, especially through isolation during World War II. With the formation of the Council of Churches in Indonesia in 1950, relationships between Protestants and Roman Catholics have become close, with consultation on evangelization, common liturgy and new marriage laws. The Council of Churches is the only council which has the goal of one Christian Church written into its constitution. Since 1966, both Roman Catholics and Protestants are registering obvious increases in adherents, in part because all citizens are obliged to belong formally to one of the four authorized and recognized religious groups (Islam, Protestantism, Catholicism, "Hindu-Buddhism").

Partisipasi (participation) continues to be a key word for the churches, expressing their commitment to the development of the nation. This shows itself in a programme for young Christians who work for a few years in Indonesian villages — many of them in remote areas — to familiarize people with intermediate technological achievements, helping them to solve their own development problems.

Other responsibilities include ministering to newly settled communities due to government policies of transmigration and caring for political prisoners. The number of Indonesian pastors who become missionaries to Europe and North America is increasing; relationships with mission boards and partner churches are evolving in new ways and international church bodies enjoy the stimulation of a growing Indonesian presence.

Association of Indonesian Baptist Churches
Batak Christian Community Church
Christian Church of East Java
Christian Churches of Java
Christian Church in Mid-Sulawesi
Christian Church of South Sulawesi
Christian Church of Sumba
Christian Evangelical Church in Minhasa
Christian Protestant Church in Indonesia
Church of Nias
Evangelical Christian Church in Bolaang-Mongondow
Evangelical Christian Church in West Irian
Evangelical Church of Sangir Talaud
Free Methodist Church – Indonesia
The Indonesian Christian Church
Kalimantan Evangelical Church
Karo Batak Protestant Church
Pasundan Christian Church
Protestant Christian Batak Church
Protestant Christian Church of Bali
Protestant Church in Indonesia
Protestant Church of the Moluccas
Protestant Church of Western Indonesia
Protestant Evangelical Church in Timor
Roman Catholic Church in Indonesia
Salvation Army
Simalungun Protestant Christian Church
Toraja Church

Include in your prayers all ecumenical councils and working groups at local or national level

Remember also all Christian movements and communities which seek to proclaim and serve Jesus Christ

For Prayer and Intercession

Give thanks . . .   for the faith, self-reliance and witness of churches in Indonesia;
for Christians' contribution to nation-building and national unity;
for the service of the churches to the poor and the prisoners,
their work of rehabilitation and relief.

Pray . . .   that the efforts of churches to grow in unity may be fullfilled
and that they may help to overcome problems presented by
ethnic and linguistic differences;
that Christians may continue to uphold integrity and truth, and
help the nation succeed in its struggle against corruption;
that Christians may truly be a community for the people,
faithful and imaginative in their ministries and sensitive and
generous in their relations with people of other faiths and per-
suasions.

Prayers . . .   Strengthen, Lord, the witness of your Church in Indonesia, that
through its ministry men, women and children may be led to
wholeness and unity to a just and peaceful future that spells
your glory.

Adelbert Sitompul and Fred Kaan

FORGIVE US THE WRONG WE HAVE DONE,
AS WE HAVE FORGIVEN THOSE WHO HAVE WRONGED US.
    When forgiveness is locked behind bared teeth
    When resentment hides behind an affable mask
    To forgive and to love are but inflated currency
    on the stock exchange of deceitful good manners.
    Wilt thou come to avenge or to forgive?
    Wilt thou come to strike down in vengeance
    or to lift up with a kiss?

Fridoline Ukur

For your own notes

Australia and New Zealand

The churches of *Australia* grew out of the country's colonial history. The first fleet in 1788 brought convicts and a chaplain. Until 1836 the Church of England enjoyed privileges not granted to other churches and the Roman Catholic Church suffered under limitations which obtained in Britain until 1829. A number of great pioneering churchmen laid the foundations for the various churches. Education, expansion, polemic and temperance societies were major preoccupations of the 19th-century churches, indeed, temperance societies were havens for early ecumenical encounter.

Today the major church is the Anglican. The Roman Catholic Church is large and the new Uniting Church in Australia, formed in June, 1977, by the Congregationalists, Methodists and Presbyterians, will certainly make an important difference to the climate of inter-church life. The strength of the Lutheran Church is mainly in South Australia. Twentieth-century patterns of migration have brought the presence of a rapidly growing community of members of the Orthodox family of churches, especially in the last 25 years.

The churches in *New Zealand* have a slightly shorter history and were spared the grim era of convict transportation that marked the first fifty years of Australia. The major denomination is again the Anglican Church, to which 40 % of the population belong. A quarter of New Zealanders are Presbyterians; the Roman Catholics and the Methodists are next in strength.

Since 1946 there has been an Australian Council of Churches and from 1941 a New Zealand Council of Churches. The major preoccupations differ slightly, while both give high priority to the development responsibilities of their relatively affluent countries. In Australia the churches' responsibilities for the aboriginal people are important. In New Zealand the Maori people have had a qualitatively different history, but today the churches are being challenged to respond to the needs of the largest Polynesian population in the Pacific and the question of Pacific-island migrant workers in New Zealand has become prominent.

Churches in both Australia and New Zealand have grown out of the 19th-century missionary impulse and shared in it. Australian and New Zealand mission boards have supported and continue to support churches in the Pacific and share, through their membership in the Christian Conference of Asia and the World Council of Churches, in wider inter-church aid programmes. Ecumenical work with the Roman Catholic Church has grown since 1967; an Action for World Development programme was set up in Australia, supported by both the Australian Council of Churches and the Roman Catholic Episcopal Conference.

Anglican Church of Australia
Associated Churches of Christ in New Zealand
Baptist Church of Australia
Baptist Union of New Zealand
Church of the Province of New Zealand
Churches of Christ in Australia
Congregational Union of New Zealand
Fellowship of Congregational Churches in Australia
Lutheran Church of Australia
Lutheran Church of New Zealand
Methodist Church of New Zealand
Orthodox Churches in Australia
Presbyterian Church of Australia
Presbyterian Church of New Zealand
Roman Catholic Church of Australia and New Zealand
Salvation Army
Society of Friends (Quakers)
Uniting Church in Australia

Include in your prayers all ecumenical councils and working groups at local or national level

Remember also all Christian movements and communities which seek to proclaim and serve Jesus Christ

For Prayer and Intercession

Give thanks . . .   for the churches in Australia and New Zealand, for all humble and joyful Christians who live to God's glory and for peace among their fellows;
for the Orthodox churches in diaspora as they contribute to a new society.

Pray . . .   that the Uniting Church in Australia may be blessed in its work and witness, that the joy of oneness may radiate from this new church to all others and to all people on this continent;
that inter-church cooperation may be deepened at all levels;
that the churches may work in respect and for justice with aboriginal and Maori peoples.

Prayer . . .   O Lord, by whose cross all enmity is ended,
all walls of separation broken down:
look with compassion upon the agonies
of your world, and by the power of
your Spirit make us instruments of your
peace; you who are our peace,
now and for ever.

From an Australian Christian

For your own notes

Week 40

The Pacific Islands

The Pacific contains more than 2,000 volcanic islands, singly or as archipelagos, and larger islands and groups of which New Guinea is the most significant.

First known to western explorers in the 16th century, whose followers came to exploit spices and sandalwood, the islanders are socially and economically in a time of transition. Some have recently acquired independence; others still are dependent on or integrated with an external country. Originally New Guinea was arbitrarily divided between British, Dutch and German interests, Samoa between German and American. New Caledonia was French. Later changes and exchanges occurred in which the interests and opinions of the inhabitants mattered little. American impact on the Northern Pacific area has been significant. The first hydrogen bomb test took place at Bikini Atoll, and French nuclear tests in recent years evoked strong protests from the region.

Melanesia has a population of over 3 million, including the independent state of Papua New Guinea, where traditional kingship communities centred on villages are the main social and political units. In Fiji there are about half a million. *Micronesia* is a far-flung assortment of small islands between South-East Asia and Polynesia. Basically people are farmers and fishermen. Most comprise US Trust Territories. *Polynesia*—"many islands"—extends from Hawaii (part of the USA) to New Zealand. The area includes Western Samoa, Tonga, the Cook Islands and Easter Island (a dependency of Chile).

The churches have grown from sustained missionary work in the 18th and 19th centuries. French Catholic mission societies, with ones in London of the Anglican, Methodist and Congregational traditions, and later on German and Dutch contributions have been part of the overall impact.

Some islands sent missionaries themselves, especially to Papua New Guinea, and the list of Pacific martyrs is not negligible. Cook Island missionaries implanted a tradition of songs and style of singing psalms and biblical texts in Papua. A folk church situation arose, where as a Western Samoan said: "Christianity was captured by the culture."

Methodism predominated in Tonga and Fiji, Congregationalism in Samoa, the Cook Islands and parts of the Solomons and Papua, the Presbyterians in New Hebrides. Roman Catholicism is strong in Papua and New Caledonia with a significant presence elsewhere. In Tahiti the Evangelical Church is in a majority. Anglicans are strong in the Solomon Islands and the Lutherans in Papua.

The Pacific Conference of Churches was begun in 1966 and in 1976 the Roman Catholic Conference of Bishops was elected to membership. Major concerns of the Conference are education, family problems and human development. The churches are fully involved in political questions, especially independence issues. Many of the smaller island groups are bewildered by US policy there, seeking to establish them as part of the "Commonwealth" of America on the Puerto Rico model.

The Pacific Islands

Church of the Province of Melanesia
Church of the Province of New Zealand
Congregational Christian Church in Samoa
Congregational Churches in the Mariana, Caroline and Marshall Islands
Cook Islands Christian Church
Ekalesia Niue
Evangelical Church in New Caledonia and Loyalty Isles
Evangelical Church of French Polynesia
Evangelical Lutheran Church of Papua New Guinea
Free Wesleyan Church of Tonga
Gilbert Islands Protestant Church
Methodist Church in Fiji
Methodist Church in Samoa
Methodist Church in Tonga
Nauru Protestant Church
Presbyterian Church of the New Hebrides
Roman Catholic Church in Papua New Guinea, Solomon Islands and the Pacific
Salvation Army
Tavalu Church (formerly Ellis Islands)
United Church in Papua, New Guinea and the Solomon Islands
Wabag Lutheran Church

Include in your prayers all ecumenical councils and working groups at local or national level

Remember also all Christian movements and communities which seek to proclaim and serve Jesus Christ

For Prayer and Intercession

Give thanks . . .   for the great response to the Gospel of Christ in the islands of the Pacific, for the growth of the churches and their missionary zeal;
for the earnest desire of the churches to work together for the peace and well-being of all peoples in the islands.

Pray . . .   that Christians of the Pacific may be strengthened to remain faithful to Christ in the face of rapid social changes and challenges;
for unity and cooperation between the churches, particularly in the common tasks of education and development.

Prayer . . .   God, our Heavenly Father, we draw near to thee with thankful hearts because of all thy great love for us. We thank thee most of all for the gift of thy dear Son, in whom alone we may be one. We are different one from another in race and language, in material things, in gifts, in opportunities, but each of us has a human heart, knowing joy and sorrow, pleasure and pain. We are one in our need of thy forgiveness, thy strength, thy love; make us one in our common response to thee, that bound by a common love and freed from selfish aims we may work for the good of all and the advancement of thy kingdom.
Through Jesus Christ, our Lord.

Salote, Queen of Tonga

For your own notes

Argentina, Paraguay and Uruguay

Before the Spanish conquest these countries were inhabited by indigenous groups related to the Tupi-Guarani tribes. The conquistadores did not engage in evangelization but Jesuits and Franciscans gave a vivid witness to the Guaranis.

Argentina has 25 million people, mostly of Spanish and Italian origin. It has shown a perplexing alternation between military and civilian rule, perhaps reflecting the alienation felt by large sections of the middle and working classes and tensions from the unresolved struggles for unification in the 19th century.

Mainly urban, its agricultural and industrial development was stimulated by earlier British interests. The present constitution, adopted in 1956, following the era of Peron, is essentially the same as that of 1863. Peron's brief comeback was followed by renewed military dictatorship and intensified unrest.

Churches—90% of the population is Roman Catholic—are joining their efforts for reconciliation and defence of human rights. This has helped create conditions for an improved ecumenical climate where Protestants (half a million), though enjoying religious liberty since 1810, remain a minority. Twenty-eight denominations are linked in the Argentine Federation of Evangelical Churches. Some Christians have been violently suppressed, yet more imprisoned for their views.

Paraguay has a population of 3 million, mainly of Guarani origin. It is landlocked, blocked by Bolivian jungles and never fully recovered from its bitter 19th-century war with Argentina, Brazil and Uruguay. The Chaco war in the 1930's was followed by a dictatorship. Protestants—who first came to the country in 1856—number 25,000.

For 10 years the Roman Catholics have been expressing concern for the rights of the Guarani people to health, work, education and a minimum standard of living, together with Disciples of Christ, Baptists, Mennonites and others. However, in a country where poverty is rampant, their involvement with poor Indians has brought suffering for the Christian witness there.

Uruguay has a population of 3 million, with the highest literacy rate in Latin America (95%). One essayist wrote: "Here is a country whose people do not aspire to greatness or to anything absolute, but who desire that things shall be kept in good, human proportions and that human values shall be treated with proper respect." Independent of Spain since 1825, it was once socially advanced. Its stable democracy had four objectives: justice for the poor; state ownership; reduction of religious and presidential power. Recently this approach has been eroded and social conflicts have led to military dictatorship, repression and violation of human rights. Churches do not have full freedom of expression and church periodicals have been closed. Many thousands, especially young people, have left the country. The churches have increased mutual collaboration for those in distress. Among the strongest Protestant groups are the Methodist and Pentecostal and the YMCA, but Uruguay has a long-standing anti-clerical tradition. The Federation of Evangelical Churches of Uruguay comprises 6 denominations.

Anglican Church
Argentine Evangelical Lutheran Church – Missouri Synod
Conventions of Evangelical Baptists in Argentina, Paraguay and Uruguay
Disciples of Christ in Argentina and Paraguay
Evangelical Church of the River Platea
Evangelical Methodist Church – Argentina and Uruguay
Independent Lutheran congregations
Mennonites
Pentecostal Churches in Argentina and Uruguay
Roman Catholic Church of Uruguay, Paraguay, Argentine
Salvation Army
United Evangelical Lutheran Church
Waldensian Evangelical Church of the River Plata

Include in your prayers all ecumenical councils and working groups at local or national level

Remember also all Christian movements and communities which seek to proclaim and serve Jesus Christ

For Prayer and Intercession

Give thanks . . .   for moves towards the creation of a Latin American Council of Churches;
for the courage and witness of Roman Catholics in many countries as they seek to follow new social paths;
for the growth of Pentecostal and other groups in the depressed areas of cities.

Pray . . .   for a greater ecumenical spirit to pervade the different traditions as they seek a common approach to overcome the immense problems of their countries;
for a greater reverence for the cultures and histories of indigenous peoples;
for willingness to work for more just political structures and try new associations, so all people can enjoy freedom with dignity.

Prayer . . .   O God, may your Church discover, then identify, its life with groups of people who suffer injustice and remain unheard. May your Church be the voice of the voiceless. Let your Church find them, and struggle with them, and so find the way of your cross, and the way to true responsibility.

Emilio Castro (slightly adapted)

For your own notes

Brazil

Brazil, with a population of 107 million, mainly of African and Portuguese descent, covers half the continent. Christianity first came there with the Portuguese conquest at the beginning of the 16th century, and for almost 400 years the Roman Catholic Church was the country's official church.

Abortive attempts to introduce Protestantism by French Huguenots in 1555 and by Dutch Reformed in 1624 were crushed by the colonial power. The importation of traditional African religion with the slaves, and the arrival of Protestant immigrants, did not alter the situation. Lack of religious liberty hindered Protestant missions for years and even at the end of the last century, when Church and state were separated (1889) and religious freedom guaranteed by the Constitution, the number of Protestants was small.

The remarkable impact, therefore, of Protestant churches, especially the Lutheran and Presbyterian, and particularly the rise of the Pentecostal movements, often in the large slum areas (the result of industrial development and the sudden growth of big cities), is a phenomenon which cannot be ignored.

Almost every denomination is growing fast, in a country where the population growth is the highest in the world. Protestants have played an important role in development, especially education and social work. Pentecostal churches have an increasing influence. While their emphasis on personal conversion leads to a certain indifference to unjust structures there is a growing awareness of society's problems and the need to tackle them.

Roman Catholics are still 93% of the population, and Vatican II initiated a renewal for them in the field of social and political action. The involvement of the Roman Catholic Church—officially or unofficially—in ecumenical work is one encouraging element in Brazil. A common publication of the New Testament, participation in the Ecumenical Committee on Coordination for Service, joint publications on violations of human rights, are but three examples.

A revolution of the right displaced the democratic legislative process with government by directive, with a new constitution in 1967 strengthening the powers of the Presidency. Lay people, priests and bishops of the Roman Catholic Church, who have opposed certain government actions, are today suffering for identification with the poor and oppressed people so that it is no longer possible to speak of them as a dominant power, supporting the status quo. On an institutional level the Church's remarkable development from 19 dioceses in 1900 to 210 in 1971 points to an aim to create units of a more human size.

Note should be taken of the influence of Afro-Brazilian cults, not only among the poor. Spiritism is another phenomenon and while government reports show only about 2% take part, some observers estimate almost 10 million people may be involved in spiritist meetings.

Association of Free Lutheran Churches of Brazil
Baptist Convention of Brazil
Christian Reformed Church in Brazil
Episcopal Church of Brazil
Evangelical Church of Lutheran Confession in Brazil
Evangelical Congregational Church of Brazil
Evangelical Lutheran Church of Brazil, Missouri Synod
Evangelical Pentecostal Church "Brazil for Christ"
Evangelical Reformed Church in Brazil
Free Methodist Church in Brazil
Independent Presbyterian Church of Brazil
Latin American Reformed Church
Methodist Church in Brazil
Presbyterian Church of Brazil
Roman Catholic Church of Brazil
Salvation Army

Include in your prayers all ecumenical councils and working groups at local or national level

Remember also all Christian movements and communities which seek to proclaim and serve Jesus Christ

For Prayer and Intercession

Give thanks . . .

for the wealth of Brazil, its peoples and Christians who dedicate their lives to serving God and their fellow citizens;
for the courageous struggle of many Christians in different churches for justice and human dignity for all people, especially the poor.

Pray . . .

for the people of Brazil, especially their leaders, that they might use their country's resources responsibly;
for all churches to be united in defending human rights, protecting minority ethnic groups, especially the Indian tribes of the Amazonas;
for the task of evangelism that the Gospel in all its fullness might be preached and believed with power.

Prayers . . .

Lord Jesus, take away the veil from our eyes, that we may contemplate the beauty of thy ideal. Grant to us thy power, to the end that we may be faithful partakers of the joys and sufferings of thy kingdom.
Tito de Alencar, in "The World At One In Prayer"

Lord, the world needs
    this marvellous wealth which is youth.
    Help young people!
    They possess the inexhaustible wealth of the future . . .
    Do not allow an easy life to corrupt them
    Nor difficulties to quench their spirit.
    Free them from the worst danger of all—
    That of getting used to being
    Old within themselves
    And only young on the outside.
Dom Hélder Cámara

For your own notes

People of other Faiths and Ideologies

In this prayer cycle our attention is focussed on the Christian Church—not in isolation, but in the wider context of the whole human community in which it is set. This week we think especially of those who belong to other families of faith or ideologies, e.g. Marxism; we also pray for those who profess no faith at all. They too are our brothers and sisters. For them, too, we give thanks. For them, too, we intercede in the name of him whose compassion embraces all.

In some places the Church finds itself keeping company with large numbers of people from one or more of the major faiths. In others, it is challenged by the convictions of those for whom faith of any kind is not an option. The quest for religious truth leads some persons to convictions and associations which seem bizarre or even offensive to us. At times, the Church reacts with fear or anger when it encounters zealous adherents of religious movements which deny or violate Christian convictions.

Situations vary, but recent years have seen signs of greater openness and mutual understanding between Christians and those of other faiths. For such signs we must be deeply grateful. Often the offer of dialogue will not be accepted; patience is then required to maintain the offer. Our witness to all people must be the love of Christ, which we cannot convey through feelings of hatred and prejudice.

The Fifth Assembly of the World Council of Churches said: "We cannot allow our faith, the gift of our sense of community in Jesus Christ, to add to the tensions and suspicions and hatreds that threaten to tear apart the one family of humanity. We cannot allow our faith to be abused for such demonic purposes. We must seek the wider community without compromising the true *skandalon* of the Gospel."

As you think of neighbours, near and far, who do not share your profession of faith in Jesus Christ,

First — Be thankful and celebrate the wealth of their humanity, compassion and wisdom.

Second — Repent and acknowledge that we Christians bear part responsibility for the misunderstandings of years gone by.

Third — Pray for peoples of all faiths and those of none, that we all may be given greater sensitivity to people who are "different", deeper understanding of traditions other than our own, and a strengthened determination to work together for the sake of the whole human community.

Fourth — Pray, once again and quite specifically, for the Church, that it may bear clearer witness to the faith it has received.

For Prayer and Intercession

Give thanks . . .
for the wholeness of the human family;
for people of other faiths and of none, especially those who are our friends and neighbours;
for the rich variety of human experience and the gifts we bring to one another when we meet in a spirit of acceptance and love;
for dialogue in community, a process of mutual enrichment and growing understanding;
for movements to establish and sustain the legitimate rights of persons of every religious conviction.

Pray . . .
that the Church may perform a reconciling ministry in a world divided by suspicion and misunderstanding and bring healing to those places where religious intolerance fractures human community;
that people of all faiths may be free to set forth their conviction with integrity and listen to one another in humility;
that persons who neglect their religious convictions and duties may find new hope and be strengthened to begin again;
that the Church may bear a true and loving witness to the one it calls Lord.

Prayer . . .
O bless this people, Lord, who seek their own face
under the mask and can hardly recognize it . . .
O bless this people that breaks its bond . . .
And with them, all the peoples of North and South,
of East and West,
who sweat blood and sufferings,
and see, in the midst of these millions of waves
the sea swell of the heads of my people
and grant to them warm hands that they may clasp
the earth in a girdle of brotherly hands,
beneath the rainbow of thy peace.

Léopold Sédar Senghor

For your own notes

Chile, Peru and Bolivia

Predominant indigenous populations in these areas were the Aymaras in Bolivia, the Araucanos in Chile and the Quechuas in Peru, rendered almost powerless by Spanish conquest in the 16th century and the influence of the culture, life style and religion of Spain. Later, with the formation of the independent states, Catholicism became the official religion.

About the middle and end of the 19th century, Protestant missions from Europe and America arrived, bringing a strong emphasis on education and spreading the Gospel. The churches of the historic traditions created colleges, social projects and aid organizations. At the same time, national autonomous churches (such as the Pentecostal groups) were established which, with their own particular characteristics, have given a different flavour to the response of faith brought by the others.

In *Chile* (population 10 million) 65 % of the people are of mixed Indian/Spanish descent. Christians here have in recent years shared deeply in its trials as a developing nation. Forces from the outside as well as inside, often arraying the Haves against the Have-nots, have contended for mastery in dealing with public issues. From the Christian Democrats to the Marxists and the military dictatorship the road has been a rough one. The situation has challenged churches to respond to ethical issues involving human rights, and to serve people in need. An Association of Evangelical Churches provides for cooperation among the main Protestant bodies growing out of earlier work in resettling European refugees and displaced people after World War II.

In *Peru* (population 14 million) European and mestizo are over 50%, 46 % are Indian, African, Chinese. The illiteracy level is over half. Peru was the home of an advanced Inca civilization conquered by the Spanish and a colony for 300 years. It has alternated between military and civilian rule. Beneath the surface many aspects of traditional Indian religion persist despite the rape of a culture. Over-arching all concerns is the challenge to relate the Gospel to ameliorating the poverty which burdens so many.

In *Bolivia* (population 7 million) over half are Indian. A series of dictators and political unrest have culminated in the sixteenth constitution, providing for a strong executive power, nationalization of mines and agrarian reform. As in Peru and Chile, Roman Catholicism predominates, claiming 94 % of the population.

There exist in these areas Christian movements which, in seeking a just and peaceful society, have united their efforts, breaking down barriers of language, confession and history to reflect on the Word of God and seek real possibilities of joint theological and pastoral work and action on human rights issues.

"Tell brothers and sisters around the world, that here we are learning how to live and work together, as Christians did in the first century", said one person from these local ecumenical communities.

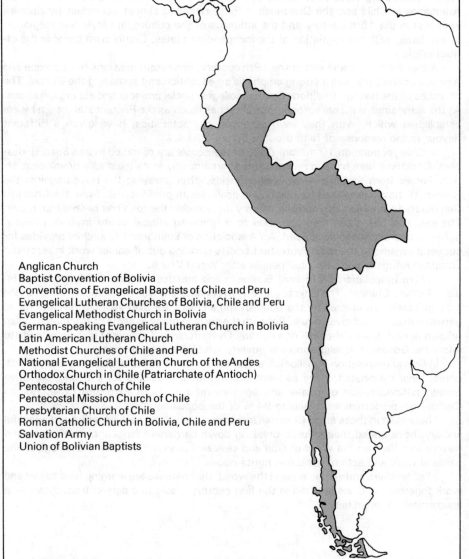

Anglican Church
Baptist Convention of Bolivia
Conventions of Evangelical Baptists of Chile and Peru
Evangelical Lutheran Churches of Bolivia, Chile and Peru
Evangelical Methodist Church in Bolivia
German-speaking Evangelical Lutheran Church in Bolivia
Latin American Lutheran Church
Methodist Churches of Chile and Peru
National Evangelical Lutheran Church of the Andes
Orthodox Church in Chile (Patriarchate of Antioch)
Pentecostal Church of Chile
Pentecostal Mission Church of Chile
Presbyterian Church of Chile
Roman Catholic Church in Bolivia, Chile and Peru
Salvation Army
Union of Bolivian Baptists

Include in your prayers all ecumenical councils and working groups at local or national level

Remember also all Christian movements and communities which seek to proclaim and serve Jesus Christ

For Prayer and Intercession

Give thanks . . . Because in Christ Christians are members of a single family, confessing one faith;
for God's Son who identified himself with humble people whom he served and loved with his life.

Pray . . . that Christians in these countries may be given strength and courage to love and serve those who are victims of injustice;
for the power to create true community, without racism or exploitation, where peace is the fruit of justice, freedom and love;
for obedience to Christ's mission, and a seeking of his will in the midst of the turbulence of contemporary society;
for the proclamation by word and deed of the Gospel of love and liberation.

Prayer . . . Prayer of the Christian Spirit (Acts 2:43-47)

Lord, is it not possible today completely
to live out your Gospel?
Are we not able to live in unity
nor to have all things in common?
When will we sell our possessions
to share them among all people,
according to the need of each one?
What are we waiting for before praying together
and in silence?
To become united in the same spirit,
to break bread in our families,
and to take this food happily,
being simple of heart,
and only praising the Lord?
Or have you asked the impossible of us,
since not every one loves us?

Fermin Cebolla Lopez

For your own notes

Week 45

Colombia, Ecuador, Venezuela, Surinam and Guyana

This area of Latin America can be divided into two distinct parts. The first, where the Roman Catholic Church is the church of the majority, consists of *Colombia* (24 million of Indian/Iberian descent), *Ecuador* (6 1/2 million) and *Venezuela* (12 million). Associated with Colombus, these countries were part of the former Spanish colonial empire which did not tolerate the existence of any other Christian community. Protestant groups were able to start mission activities, even among resident foreigners, only after the countries gained their political independence during the third decade of the 19th century. In many instances such activities were restricted until the beginning, or even the middle, of the 20th.

In the second part of the area the Guyanas (*Surinam*, formerly Dutch Guyana, and *Guyana*, formerly British Guyana and before 1815 part of Dutch Guyana) had Protestant churches established in the colonial period. Moravian work, for example, was initiated by Zinzendorf. The tolerant attitude of the 18th and 19th centuries made it possible for a great variety of traditions, including the Roman Catholic, to enter and start mission work.

As a result the Roman Catholic Church is the traditional church of both Colombia and Ecuador, and also in Venezuela in a different way, where generally a more liberal spirit, a lack of indigenous clergy and the advance of secularization and a materialistic view of life, have created a situation more similar to that of North Atlantic countries.

Most of the Protestant groups are strongly evangelical, often fundamentalist, and are critical of the Roman Catholic Church. In Colombia many Protestants cooperate in the Evangelical Confederation.

As a result, a non-institutional approach to church cooperation is followed, though there is a Council of Churches in Guyana. In spite of their enthusiastic missionary activities, the Evangelical churches have not registered much increase in their numbers in a continent where the number of young people in the population is often high. Nor, for that matter, do the more traditional Protestant churches, with their emphasis on ministering to the middle and upper-middle classes, show many signs of growth.

While the multitude of denominations may give an impression of missionary zeal, most of them remain relatively static. The presence of communities of other faiths (Muslims, Hindus and, in Surinam, Buddhists) adds to the complexity of the situation. The financial strength of traditionally Muslim countries elsewhere is reflected in the continued growth of the local Muslim communities, and the interest of westerners in the religious thought of the Indian sub-continent has contributed to the spiritual awakening and mounting self-esteem among Hindus and Buddhists in the region.

African Methodist Episcopal Church – Guyana
African Methodist Episcopal Zion Church – Guyana
Baptist Convention of Colombia
Baptist Cooperation Convention of Guyana
Church in the Province of the West Indies
Congregational Union of Guyana
Episcopal Church
Evangelical Lutheran Church in Surinam
Evangelical Lutheran Church – Colombia Synod
Federation of Evangelical Lutheran Churches of Ecuador
Guyana Presbyterian Church
Lutheran Church in Guyana
Lutheran Council of Venezuela
Methodist Church in the Caribbean and the Americas – Guyana
Moravian Church – Guyana and Surinam
National Baptist Convention of Venezuela
Presbyterian Church of Colombia
Presbyterian Church of Venezuela
Roman Catholic Church
Salvation Army
Wesleyan Church – Colombia
Wesleyan Church – Guyana

Include in your prayers all ecumenical councils and working groups at local or national level

Remember also all Christian movements and communities which seek to proclaim and serve Jesus Christ

For Prayer and Intercession

Give thanks . . .   for all true and humble Christian witness in these lands;
for ecumenical beginnings, for acts of solidarity in situations of
suffering and oppression.

Pray . . .   that all Christians may find and follow the path to God which
leads them to solidarity with the oppressed, the hungry and the
neglected;
for a deeper sense of responsibility and care to grow among the
people, especially those with great wealth;
for the churches to become a sign of healing and concord in the
midst of a polarized society;
that the ecumenical movement may become alive in all lands
and churches may grow in fellowship together.

Prayer . . .   *Lord, when did we see you?*
I was hungry and starving
    and you were obese;
Thirsty
    and you were watering your garden;
With no road to follow, and without hope
    and you called the police and were
    happy that they took me prisoner;
Barefoot and with ragged clothing
    and you were saying "I have nothing
    to wear, tomorrow I will buy something new"
Sick
    and you asked: "Is it infectious?"
Prisoner
    and you said: "That is where all those
    of your class should be"
Lord, have mercy!

For your own notes

Week 46

The Caribbean

This area comprises the greater and lesser Antilles, the Bahamas and continental off-shore islands, of which Cuba (9 million people of Spanish/African descent) is largest. In the Dominican Republic which shares an island with Haiti, the 5 million people have experienced successive dictatorships. Martinique and Guadeloupe have been ruled by France since 1635. Puerto Rico was owned by Spain till 1898; now its 3 million people are part of the USA with "commonwealth status". The Dutch Antilles consist of small islands off the mainland coast. The English-speaking West Indies comprise Jamaica, the Bahamas, Trinidad and Tobago, Barbados, and various associated states and crown colonies.

All these states' encounter with Europe goes back to Columbus as, in the 15th century, he sought a new passage to India—hence the original name "the West Indies". Besides extensive European and American involvement, the populations of the islands became remarkably diverse as a result of African, Chinese, East Indian and Portuguese slave and indentured labour which worked in the sugar plantations and other industries.

Christianity was at first confined to settlers. Then missions to slaves developed from many European traditions, especially the Anglican and Methodist. Roman Catholicism or Protestantism dominated according to who ruled. The territories now are mainly Christian, with a significant growth of new and independent churches in the last 25 years. There are also Muslims and Hindus, especially in Trinidad. Voodoo, the syncretistic African cult, is the most important religion in Haiti. Others are found elsewhere, notably in Cuba.

The political and social situations constitute very different challenges to the Church. In Cuba, the churches are trying to discern what their discipleship requires of them in a socialist society. Elsewhere churches face the questions posed by free-enterprise capitalism in one or another form. Everywhere the issue of economic justice and development is of major importance.

The blending of various peoples, cultures and races, is clearly visible in the churches, which formed the Caribbean Conference of Churches in 1973. Most Protestants and the Roman Catholic Church belong. Its purpose is clear in its Constitution: "We, as Christian people of the Caribbean, separated from each other by barriers of history, language, class and distance, desire, because of our common calling in Christ, to join together in a regional fellowship of churches for inspiration, consultation and cooperative action. We are deeply concerned to promote human liberation of our people, and are committed to the achievement of human justice and the dignity of man in society. We desire to build up together our life in Christ and to share our experiences with the universal brotherhood of mankind."

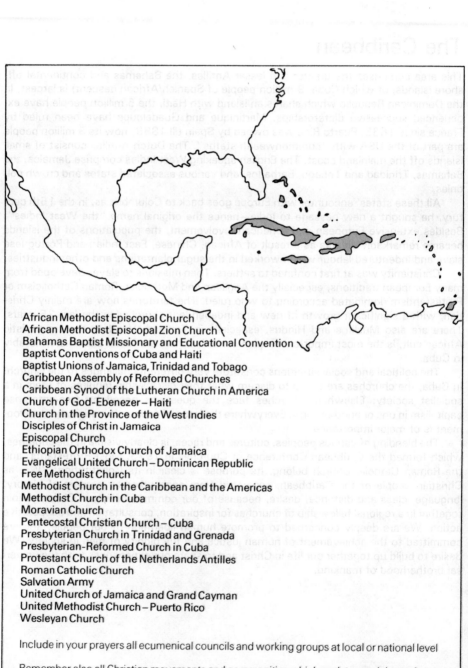

African Methodist Episcopal Church
African Methodist Episcopal Zion Church
Bahamas Baptist Missionary and Educational Convention
Baptist Conventions of Cuba and Haiti
Baptist Unions of Jamaica, Trinidad and Tobago
Caribbean Assembly of Reformed Churches
Caribbean Synod of the Lutheran Church in America
Church of God-Ebenezer – Haiti
Church in the Province of the West Indies
Disciples of Christ in Jamaica
Episcopal Church
Ethiopian Orthodox Church of Jamaica
Evangelical United Church – Dominican Republic
Free Methodist Church
Methodist Church in the Caribbean and the Americas
Methodist Church in Cuba
Moravian Church
Pentecostal Christian Church – Cuba
Presbyterian Church in Trinidad and Grenada
Presbyterian-Reformed Church in Cuba
Protestant Church of the Netherlands Antilles
Roman Catholic Church
Salvation Army
United Church of Jamaica and Grand Cayman
United Methodist Church – Puerto Rico
Wesleyan Church

Include in your prayers all ecumenical councils and working groups at local or national level

Remember also all Christian movements and communities which seek to proclaim and serve Jesus Christ

For Prayer and Intercession

Give thanks . . .   for the growth of the faith in Jesus Christ in the Caribbean;
for the unity of the churches as expressed in the Caribbean
Conference of Churches;
for the development and renewal work of the Caribbean Conference of Churches as it strives to liberate Caribbean people
from injustice and to lead them into the joy of Christian
fellowship.

Pray . . .   for peace and tranquility in the island world of the Caribbean as
its people move towards greater self-determination and independence;
for the Caribbean Conference of Churches that increasingly it
may be the instrument of unity, mission and service;
for young people and children in the Caribbean many of whom
have to live without a stable family.

Prayer . . .   The right hand of God is striking in our land
Striking out at envy, hate and greed.
Our selfishness and lust, our pride and deeds unjust
Are destroyed by the right hand of God.
The right hand of God is healing in our land,
Healing broken bodies, minds and souls.
So wondrous is its touch,
With love that means so much,
When we're healed by the right hand of God.
The right hand of God is planting in our land,
Planting seeds of freedom, hope and love.
In these Caribbean lands
Let his people all join hands
And be one with the right hand of God.

Patrick Prescod

197

For your own notes

Week 47

Mexico and Central America: Belize, Costa Rica, El Salvador, Guatemala, Honduras, Nicaragua, Panama

The 1,200-mile long mountainous land bridge joining North and South America lying between *Mexico* and *Colombia* includes *Guatemala, El Salvador, Belize, Honduras, Nicaragua, Costa Rica* and *Panama and the Canal Zone.*

Its combined population is about 20 million and predominantly mestizo—a mingling of Amerindian and European stock with African elements.

The Spanish conquistadores brought the cross of Christ to Central America and to Mexico. Since then, the Roman Catholic Church has been in the majority. Many missionaries and bishops have identified themselves selflessly with the indigenous people. But for the greater part of the region's history in the past four centuries, the Roman Catholic Church has been on the side of the ruling establishment. When the countries became independent, there was a strong sense of anti-clericalism and, as in the case of the Mexican revolution in the 19th century, severe attacks on the Church.

The Protestant churches are very small. They arrived either with the European settlers or with missionaries from the United States. Generally speaking, the Protestant churches follow a conservative and even fundamentalist tradition. There is some native leadership and a limited amount of cooperation among them. Similarly, cooperation with the Roman Catholic Church is marginal, but it is increasing day by day, especially in Christian service together in response to the social-political-economic reality of the region. Nevertheless, there are efforts to bring Christians together: the Christian Council of Mexico, the Evangelical Committee for Help to Development (CEPAD) in Nicaragua and the Central American Evangelical Regional Committee are just three examples of national and regional cooperation.

Central America is severely divided. This applies not only to the ecclesiastical situation but also to politics and international relations, with serious tensions existing between, for instance, Honduras and El Salvador, Guatemala and Belize. With the exception of Costa Rica, all governments are under direct military rule or dependent on military power. Mexico has a one-party government. Human rights get little support in most countries, and least so in Nicaragua.

The social and economic situation is rapidly deteriorating. As a result, the poor suffer most. The cleavage between the few who are wealthy and the many who are needy is growing. Wherever there are clusters of indigenous people, they are usually treated as second-class citizens. In all these countries church leaders, specially Roman Catholics, are suffering for their obedience to the Gospel. Some have paid with death for their testimonies.

Baptist Association of El Salvador
Baptist Conventions of Costa Rica, Honduras, Guatemala, Panama and Nicaragua
Council of Lutheran Churches in Central America and Panama
Episcopal Church
Evangelical Methodist Church of Costa Rica
Independent Lutheran Congregations
Lutheran Synod of Mexico
Methodist Church in Costa Rica, Panama and Honduras/Belize
Methodist Church of Mexico
Mexican Lutheran Church
National Baptist Convention of Mexico
National Evangelical Presbyterian Church of Guatemala
Pentecostal Churches in these countries
Primative Methodist Church – Guatemala
Roman Catholic Church
Salvation Army
United Methodist Church – Costa Rica
Wesleyan Church – Honduras/Belize, and Mexico

Include in your prayers all ecumenical councils and working groups at local or national level

Remember also all Christian movements and communities which seek to proclaim and serve Jesus Christ

For Prayer and Intercession

Give thanks . . .
for humble and committed Christians past and present who have put their love of God to the service of their fellow human beings;
for Christians and action groups who struggle for the liberation of the needy and oppressed, for their witness to the human rights of all.

Pray . . .
for unity and solidarity within churches, between groups of committed Christians and the ecclesiastical leadership;
that the churches may struggle together for the needs of every citizen, for the improvement of social and educational conditions, especially of the poor, children and young people;
for unity and cooperation among the countries of Central America and for peaceful development and the protection of human rights.

Prayer . . .
Free us, Lord,
because their parties did not free us.
They fool each other,
They exploit each other.
Their lies are repeated by thousands of radios,
Their slanders by every newspaper,
They have special workshops for making up those lies.
Those who say
"We shall dominate by means of propaganda,
Propaganda is with us."

"Because of the oppression of the poor
Because of the groans of the exploited
I will arise now"
Says the Lord,
"I will give them freedom because they sigh"
But the words of the Lord are clean words
They are not propaganda.

Ernesto Cardenal

For your own notes

Week 48

United States of America (1)

Four Roman Catholic priests landed with a party of Spanish *conquistadores*, establishing the first permanent Christian mission in the "new world" on the feast of St. Augustine, 1565.

During the next four centuries, the area that was to become the USA received waves of immigrants mostly from Europe, but also sizable immigration from Asia and Latin America, and slaves brought from Africa.

Each immigrant group had its own expressions of faith. Among Christians, this resulted in a plurality of church structures: Roman Catholic, Lutheran, Reformed, Methodist, Episcopal, Baptist, Quaker, Congregational, Moravian, and several churches of the Orthodox family. Often national or ethnic origins influenced the creation of separate denominations within a confessional family. Political and regional loyalties also divided churches. The Civil War split many churches. Some of these divisions have healed; others over a century later are still in the process of healing.

Black churches in the U.S. have not only been influenced by ethnic heritage, but in the face of centuries of experience with slavery and segregation, have been profoundly marked by their struggles for freedom and equality. Many new churches have arisen, some becoming large bodies, like the Christian Church (Disciples of Christ), the independent Churches of Christ, the Church of the Latter Day Saints, the Christian Science Church, and more recently, the Pentecostal unions.

Other religions have also taken root. Judaism has been profoundly influenced by immigration patterns. In the 20th century, Buddhism, Hinduism, and Islam are also present as communities of faith.

Christianity has been predominant, but there is no state church. The pluralism of religious expression in the United States by the time the young government wrote its Constitution, combined with a vision of religious freedom contributed by the left-wing of the Reformation, resulted in a revolutionary decision for religious freedom. The Bill of Rights of the U.S. Constitution guarantees that "Congress shall make no law respecting an establishment of religion, or prohibiting the free exercise thereof." This separation of Church and state has meant that each church depends on its own vitality and faithfulness for growth.

Though large-scale immigration has ended, the church in the "American melting-pot" has been able to help preserve language and customs from the countries of origin. Today the challenge for the churches in the United States is to achieve a style of unity that conserves the unique contributions of the various heritages, yet brings people together across cultural, racial and economic barriers as one living, proclaiming and serving church.

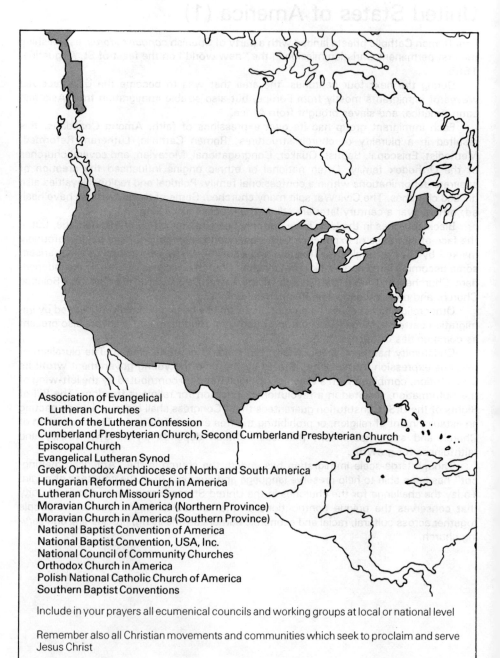

Association of Evangelical
    Lutheran Churches
Church of the Lutheran Confession
Cumberland Presbyterian Church, Second Cumberland Presbyterian Church
Episcopal Church
Evangelical Lutheran Synod
Greek Orthodox Archdiocese of North and South America
Hungarian Reformed Church in America
Lutheran Church Missouri Synod
Moravian Church in America (Northern Province)
Moravian Church in America (Southern Province)
National Baptist Convention of America
National Baptist Convention, USA, Inc.
National Council of Community Churches
Orthodox Church in America
Polish National Catholic Church of America
Southern Baptist Conventions

Include in your prayers all ecumenical councils and working groups at local or national level

Remember also all Christian movements and communities which seek to proclaim and serve
Jesus Christ

For Prayer and Intercession

Give thanks . . .   for the vitality of the people of many churches, traditions and cultures who have settled in the USA;
for the courage of Christian men and women who have not only claimed religious freedom for themselves but have also advocated it for others.

Pray . . .   for churches which use their freedom as an excuse for isolation or self-centredness;
that the measure of freedom given to the US churches may inspire them to seek a new unity, as bold and radical now as was the notion of religious liberty 200 years ago.

Prayer . . .   O God, who has bound us together in this bundle of life, give us grace to understand how our lives depend upon the courage, the industry, the honesty and the integrity of our fellow men, that we may be mindful of their needs, grateful for their faithfulness, and faithful in our responsibilities to them; through Jesus Christ our Lord.

Reinhold Niebuhr

For your own notes

United States of America (2)

Besides securing new territory, the Spanish *conquistadores* who first explored the Americas were commissioned to win the indigenous population to Roman Catholicism. The mission churches across the south and southwest of the United States today witness to the evangelizing purpose which was part of their conquest.

It was not just the native peoples whom they sought to evangelize. In 1800, fewer than 10% of the citizens of European heritage were members of congregations. Churches were rare on the American frontier, so their primary commitment was to win converts and establish new congregations. Hence, revivalism marked their life in the first century of the nation's history, taking a variety of forms in different denominations and regions as a Gospel of personal salvation was preached with intensity and persuasion.

The churches in the United States today remain centred in congregational worship, where the Good News is proclaimed in Word and Sacrament, calling individuals to repentance and renewal of faith. Sunday schools and church-related schools provide Christian education and nurture.

Yet, Christian witness has not been solely concerned with individual salvation, but often at critical points has called the nation to repentance. From the abolition of slavery to the ending of war in Vietnam, the testimony of Christians and the resolve of the churches have been crucial. A prominent witness to structures of oppression in our time was Martin Luther King, a Baptist minister. He led a challenge which has inspired people everywhere to combat injustice.

The churches, too, have been important agencies for responding to basic needs. The Roman Catholic, Lutheran, and Orthodox churches have played a special role in shepherding new arrivals to the United States and serving their welfare. Church missions in every city, notably those of the Salvation Army, have provided Christian love in very tangible forms to people in need. Pastoral counselling centres aid the distressed, and church-owned hospitals care for the ill. Church benevolent centres are homes for homeless children and older people.

In addition, Christians of the United States have given generously of people and money to carry the Gospel everywhere. They have rejoiced in the development of young churches around the world and many are now discovering new forms of enriching relationships with the world Christian family.

For all its contributions, the church remains a very human institution, easily tempted to self-interest. But its severest critics have always been within the Christian community, speaking both of Christ's love and his call through judgment to new life.

Lutheran Church in America
Lutheran Churches of the Reformation
Presbyterian Church in the United States
Progressive National Baptist Convention
Protestant Conference (Lutheran)
Reformed Church in America
Religious Society of Friends
Roman Catholic Church in the United States
Salvation Army
Seventh Day Baptist General Conference
United Church of Christ
United Methodist Church
United Presbyterian Church in the USA
Wisconsin Evangelical Lutheran Synod

Include in your prayers all ecumenical councils and working groups at local or national level

Remember also all Christian movements and communities which seek to proclaim and serve Jesus Christ

For Prayer and Intercession

Give thanks . . .

for those who have had the courage to live in conflict when that was the way of Christ;
for those with courage to reconcile when that, too, was the way of Christ;
for those who serve Christ's Church in quiet and unnoticed ways.

Pray . . .

for those who proclaim the Gospel, teach the Good News;
for those who tend the sick, care for children and serve those most in need;
for those who are advocates for the poor, struggle for justice and challenge oppression.

Prayer . . .

Eternal God, whose image lies in the hearts of all people, I find myself a sojourner among a people whose ways are strange to me, whose faith is foreign to me, whose tongue is unintelligible to me. Help me to remember that these, too, are your people, who you love with a great love, that all religion is in some way an attempt to respond to you, that the yearnings of these hearts are much like my own, and are known to you. O you who were here long before I came, help me to recognize you in the words of truth, the things of beauty, the actions of love about me. I pray through Christ, who is a stranger to no one land more than to another, and to every land no less than to another.

Robert H. Adams Jr.

For your own notes

United States of America (3)

Participation by *United States* churches in the ecumenical movement began at the turn of this century. Mission societies from the US were well represented at the Edinburgh Missionary Conference in 1910, a milestone event for the modern ecumenical movement. The Church in the United States provided leadership and resources to the International Missionary Council and to both the Faith and Order and the Life and Work movements. Twenty-eight US churches were among the founding members of the World Council of Churches in 1948.

Several ventures in inter-church cooperation at the national level were united in 1950 in the National Council of Churches of Christ in the United States of America. The NCC has served as a vital programme resource for member churches and an effective forum through which to come to terms with contemporary social issues. Regional, state and metropolitan councils have also been organized for cooperation and programme in relation to area, state and urban concerns. Church Women United brings together women from Roman Catholic, Protestant and Orthodox traditions.

A dramatic sermon preached in 1960 by Eugene Carson Blake, then Stated Clerk of the United Presbyterian Church in the USA, in San Francisco's Grace Cathedral (Episcopal), called for negotiations leading to a union of churches in the United States. This challenge captured the imagination of many and in 1962 the Consultation on Church Union (COCU) was launched with four churches taking part. Many others joined, including three black churches. The participating churches now number ten.

The ecumenical life in the United States has been enriched by the new possibilities for dialogue and cooperation with the Roman Catholic Church emerging from the Vatican Council. The spirit of *aggiornamento* brought the Roman Catholic Church into the mainstream of ecumenical initiatives and leadership. Parallel to the emerging theological consensus reflected in COCU has been the continuation of bilateral conversations between churches and confessional families. Roman Catholic, Lutheran and Orthodox churches have been prominent in the development of such dialogues.

In the 1970's a new form of ecumenical activity has emerged cutting across denominational lines through such movements as feminism, liberation theology, charismatic renewal and the evangelical revival. Ecumenism in the United States, through diverse forms, continues to bring the churches together in proclamation and service.

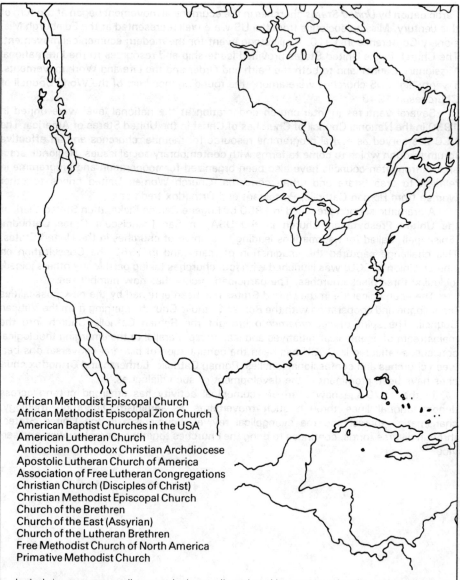

African Methodist Episcopal Church
African Methodist Episcopal Zion Church
American Baptist Churches in the USA
American Lutheran Church
Antiochian Orthodox Christian Archdiocese
Apostolic Lutheran Church of America
Association of Free Lutheran Congregations
Christian Church (Disciples of Christ)
Christian Methodist Episcopal Church
Church of the Brethren
Church of the East (Assyrian)
Church of the Lutheran Brethren
Free Methodist Church of North America
Primative Methodist Church

Include in your prayers all ecumenical councils and working groups at local or national level

Remember also all Christian movements and communities which seek to proclaim and serve Jesus Christ

For Prayer and Intercession

Give thanks . . .   for the unity of the Church which is God's gift to us in Jesus Christ;
for the churches of the USA which have already united and for the Consultation on Church Union.

Pray . . .   for God's grace to heal the festering divisions between peoples and histories;
for all Christian agencies seeking to bring US churches closer together in new ministries and patterns of life and work;
for a strengthening of the theological, social and personal contributions of American Christians to the life of the Church universal.

Prayer . . .   O Risen Christ, you made yourself known to the disciples in the breaking of the bread at Emmaus; the bread we break at this table is a sign of the brokenness of all the world; through our sharing in the Bread of Life in our many Christian communions, open our eyes and hands to the needs of all people. Let our hearts burn to share your gifts and help us to go forth together with Bread: Bread of Hope, Bread of Life, Bread of Peace.
Prepared by an ecumenical committee for the Participation of Christians of Other Churches in the 41st Eucharistic Congress, 1976, Philadelphia, Pennsylvania.

For your own notes

Canada

The first Christians in *Canada* came from Europe in the 15th century, possibly earlier, in search of fish, furs and spices. Churches were established by settlers who arrived with early explorers—Roman Catholics from France; Anglicans, Methodists and Presbyterians from Britain. Other bodies were formed from successive waves of immigration, mainly from Europe and Asia. Recently large numbers from the Caribbean have enlarged the Muslim, Hindu and Buddhist communities in some urban centres.

In a population of about 23 million the Roman Catholic Church, of nearly 10 million, is the largest. The United Church of Canada reaches about 2 million and the Anglican Church of Canada, 1 million. Baptists, Lutherans, Orthodox, Pentecostals, Presbyterians, include between 150,000 and 300,000 each.

Canadians and their churches are struggling with deep-rooted and far-reaching challenges especially in the light of the call for separation by the people and government of Quebec province. The churches are assisting this intense national dialogue which will have implications for future immigration, transportation and industrial development policies, and for the total life of the churches themselves.

An equally serious challenge to the churches is the discovery of the rightful place of the original peoples of Canada in the development and life of the country. Ecumenical programmes lend support to the struggle for aboriginal rights, opposition to the McKenzie Valley pipeline and encourage dialogue with the Indian and Eskimo populations about their traditional religion.

There is growing ecumenical collaboration in other concerns too—an annual Ten Days for World Development, a struggle against investments in South Africa, a fight for human rights and a welcome for refugees from countries like Chile. In these and traditional questions of faith and order, the Canadian Council of Churches, local councils, and the Roman Catholic Church, have developed ways of working together. Member churches of the Canadian Council of Churches, the Roman Catholic Church and some others are also working on a new national ecumenical association of churches.

For the larger churches the understanding of "mission" has become more and more a concept of partnership. While Canadians serve with churches in other countries, a growing number of pastors, teachers of theology and lay people from Africa, Asia and Latin America, add strength to the churches in Canada.

Anglican Church of Canada
Armenian Orthodox Church
Baptist Federation of Canada
Canadian Yearly Meeting of the Society of Friends
Christian Church (Disciples of Christ)
Coptic Orthodox Church
Evangelical Lutheran Church of Canada
Free Methodist Church
Greek Orthodox Church
Lutheran Church in America – Canada Section
Lutheran Church – Canada
Presbyterian Church in Canada
Reformed Church in America
Roman Catholic Church in Canada
Salvation Army
United Church of Canada
The Wesleyan Church

Include in your prayers all ecumenical councils and working groups at local or national level

Remember also all Christian movements and communities which seek to proclaim and serve Jesus Christ

For Prayer and Intercession

Give thanks . . .

for the riches and abundance of the land in Canada;
for the apostolic zeal with which the Gospel was proclaimed in the "new world";
for the willingness of people to hear the Gospel and live as its witnesses;
for the growing sense of stewardship among those to whom much is given;
for the ecumenical thrusts which seek to reconcile the separated churches and peoples of Canada.

Pray . . .

for those who serve the needs of people in Canada;
for reconciliation between French and English;
for movements seeking solidarity with Indian and Eskimo people and with the urban poor;
for all who share ecumenical work at local, regional and national levels;
for those who bring the Gospel to bear on the lives of people with a fresh call to renewal.

Prayer . . .

for mutual understanding:
Heavenly Father, in your Son, Jesus Christ, you revealed to us the way, the truth and the life. Through him, you commanded us to love one another.
In him, may we find, all of us, — citizens of different origins, in a rapidly changing Canada — guidance, inspiration, confidence!
May your Spirit lead us to practise mutual respect; may he help us to understand and to support one another!
Strengthened by your help, with daring and perseverance, may we build together,
for the common good of our fellow-citizens, a new society founded on truth, justice and love!

Irenee Beaubien

For your own notes

Week 52

The Communion of Saints in Adoration of God

In the course of the annual cycle, we have discovered the existence of Christian communities very different from our own. We have thanked God for them and for the faith in the Lord Jesus Christ which we share. As we have prayed, we have been sensitized to the wholeness of the Church, and we have newly committed ourselves to the fellowship of all God's people.

It is a very great experience to belong to the Church universal which is spread out over the whole earth. It is a source of deep joy to know that we are included in the prayers of all God's family.

The small child wonders how God can hear all the prayers at once, and we do not know how to answer. It is a mystery. Here is a greater mystery still: God hears not only the intercessions of those who walk the earth this moment but also the appeals of the faithful of all generations. Week by week, as we have read about the history of the Church and its growth across the world, we have experienced the invisible community of those who have preceded us on the way. In our prayers we commune with the martyrs, confessors and faithful of the past and present, and we rejoice that we are never alone in the kingdom of God. St. John Chrysostom wrote, "When I fall down, thousands with me fall that moment. And when I rise, others too follow me."

We rejoice in the universal Church, a fellowship which transcends time and space and which draws us together across barriers of culture and race. We praise God for the reconciling ministry of his Holy Spirit who calls us to an awareness of the communion of the saints. We savour this foretaste of God's kingdom, of life in the fullness of faith, hope and love.

As we move into a new year of prayer and dedication we put our trust in God who alone is trustworthy and reliable. We do not know what the future holds in store for the Church and the world, but with the Apostle Paul we glorify God in saying:

"If God is on our side, who is against us? . . ."

(Rom. 8:31-39)

For Prayer and Intercession

Give thanks . . .

for the creation of a world full of rich variety within the human family;
for the life of the Church around the world;
for the faithful disciples of every generation;
for the confessors and martyrs who could not be made to deny their faith;
for the communion of saints which transcends time and space.

Pray . . .

for the Church, at least a foretaste of your new creation;
that it may fulfil in growing measure the purposes you intend for it;
that it may willingly give itself to be guided by the Holy Spirit;
that your love may be so apparent in its life that no one can deny its witness to your healing love in all creation;
that all who come in humility and faith may live in the constant awareness of the communion of saints in whose company we intercede for all who offer a true witness in every time and place.

Prayer . . .

God our Father, source of all holiness, the work of your hands is manifest in your saints, the beauty of your truth is reflected in their faith.
May we who aspire to have part in their joy be filled with the Spirit that blessed their lives, so that having shared their faith on earth we may also know their peace in your kingdom.
Grant this through Christ our Lord.

The Roman Missal

For your own notes

How to use the Ecumenical Prayer Cycle

Suggestions for Worship

Introduction

It may be that you will find it most convenient to share in prayer for all God's people as part of your personal devotions or those of a prayer circle or Bible-study group that meets in your neighbourhood or place of work. If so, the opportunities open to you are as far-reaching as your own imagination. But it is also hoped that local churches will use this book in some regular, meaningful way, so the rest of this chapter contains suggestions about ways in which the ecumenical cycle of prayer might be used in the liturgical life and other activities of congregations.

Naturally, different churches will employ different methods when praying for their fellow Christians around the globe. And no book of this size could provide models that would meet the needs of each participating congregation. So a good deal of sensitivity and imagination will be needed on the part of priests, pastors and parish worship committees in order to adapt the contents of this prayer cycle to the particular requirements of their congregations. But this task can be performed, and the suggestions which follow (based on Week 35, churches in India) show techniques for incorporating prayers for different churches into existing worship patterns.

1. Set Prayers for the Church and the World in Traditional Language

A number of churches which celebrate the Eucharist according to a written form, and in "traditional" language, use a prayer for the Church and the world which is derived from, or akin to, the "Prayer for the Whole State of Christ's Church" in *The Book of Common Prayer* of the Church of England. Although interpolations into a prayer of this kind need to be made with care—and with sensitivity to language—there are a number of possibilities, of which the following is just one example (the added words are underlined):

> . . . Give grace, O heavenly Father, to all Bishops and Curates, that they may both by their life and doctrine set forth thy true and lively Word, and rightly and duly administer thy holy Sacraments. *Pour forth thy blessing, O Lord, upon thy churches in India, which for centuries have been a sign of hope to the despairing, that with burning zeal and love they may bear faithful witness unto thee, and diligently proclaim thy glory, to the building up of thy Church and the salvation of souls.* And to all thy people give thy heavenly grace; and specially to this congregation here present; that with meek heart and due reverence. . .

2. Traditional Litanies

Other churches which worship in a traditional style formulate the prayers of the faithful in a litany, the phrasing of whose intentions is more or less fixed. A number of them, churches of the Reformation as well as Orthodox churches, make use of the Great Litany from the Liturgy of St John Chrysostom, and some may find it appropriate to insert into it, after the clause which asks prayers for the clergy and people, a petition directly related to the concern of the week. Again, sensitivity to language and form is important. For example:

Leader	For the leaders of our churches, for their councils, and for the diaconate which is in Christ, for the whole clergy and people, let us pray to the Lord.
People	Kyrie eleison.
Leader	*For the churches of (India), and for all who pray with us in this holy hour, and at every season; for their zeal, labour and earnestness, let us pray to the Lord.*
People	Kyrie eleison.
Leader	For all heads of state and for all governments, let us pray to the Lord.
People	Kyrie eleison.

3. Modern Litanies

Then there are churches which use a litany employing the language of everyday speech. These have been cast in a variety of forms and often a great deal of flexibility is allowed in the shaping of the litany's petitions. Much creativity and imagination can be used in adapting this prayer form to the ecumenical prayer cycle for use in the services of different churches. In the first of the following examples more than one voice can be used in leading the various parts of the litany.

Leader 1	For the Church spread throughout the world, that it may be gathered together in unity to the glory of your Name, we pray:
People	Make us one in your love. (silence may follow here and elsewhere for private prayer)
Leader 2	We give you thanks, O Lord, for the unity you have given to your Church; help all Christian people to be aware of what we already share in common and make them burn with desire to be more completely one, for your Name's sake.
People	Amen.
Leader 1	In thanksgiving for the mission you have entrusted to the Christian churches of India, to identify themselves with their fellow citizens in tasks of nation-building, and to maintain a dialogue with their non-Christian brothers and sisters for the sake of creating a truly human society founded on justice and peace, we pray:
People	Make us one in your love.

224

Leader 2	O Lord, strengthen those dedicated to serving the Gospel of your Son, so that all who confess your Name may unite in your truth and live together in your love and peace.
People	Amen.
Leader 1	For all those who govern the nations, and in particular the governments and heads of state in the Indian subcontinent, that they may find humane and agreeable solutions to the problems facing their peoples, we pray:
People	Make us one in your love. . . .

The second example has a somewhat simpler format. Here, too, the leading of it might be shared among several members of the congregation.

Leader	God, you have strengthened your people in hope. Therefore, we pray:
People	Lord, you are the hope of your people.
Leader	We pray for the Church scattered throughout the world, and we remember especially today our brothers and sisters in the churches in India, that we and they may be sanctified in your Name.
People	Lord, you are the hope of your people.
Leader	Lord, we thank you for such people as Gandhi and Mother Teresa who, while coming from different backgrounds, cultures and religions, have given new hope to the people of India and to all humankind.
People	Lord, you are the hope of your people.
Leader	Lord, we pray that more and more Indians will hear your word and your call to service in the churches, so that they may aid the cause of building a just and humane society in their country.
People	Lord, you are the hope of your people. . . .

4. Collects

A wide variety of churches find most suitable to their needs that form of prayer often known as the "collect"—used at the Eucharist and in the daily offices of Matins or Lauds, and Evensong, Vespers or Compline. In such cases the prayer related to the special concern of the week would come in the groups of collects that follow the appointed collect of the day.

A general collect, adapted from an ancient prayer and retaining its archaic style, might serve the purpose, or a modern version of an ancient collect might be preferred. For example:

Almighty and everliving God, by whose Spirit
the whole body of thy faithful people
is governed and sanctified:

receive our supplications and prayers
which we offer before thee
for all members of thy holy Church
throughout the whole world.
We remember especially before thee today
the churches of India.
We pray that in their life and ministry
they may truly and faithfully serve thee;
through our Lord and Saviour Jesus Christ.

Almighty and eternal God,
your Spirit guides the Church
and makes it holy.
Hear our prayers
for every member of the Body of Christ
everywhere in the world.
Today we remember in particular
the churches of India
and their centuries of loving witness to your truth.
By the power of your Spirit
help them to do your work
with faithfulness and devotion.
We ask this through Christ our Lord.

The underlined words are, of course, variable, according to the week of the ecumenical prayer cycle, and may be expanded to include particular churches and petitions, but it should be remembered that collects are characterized by their brevity and terseness of language.

Instead of an adapted collect, it would also be possible to compose a new collect based on the petitions "For Prayer and Intercession" of the particular week. There will also be cases when a prayer from the particular region will itself be a collect or, like Sarah Chakko's beautifully simple prayer in Week 35, eminently suitable for use with the collect of the day.

5. Exhortations to Prayer and Pastoral Prayers

There are some churches which will prefer to remember their fellow Christians elsewhere in the world by means of an exhortation to prayer. This is particularly appropriate in congregations that have periods of silence in their worship or encourage spontaneous acts of devotion from members of the gathered fellowship. Such an exhortation might be as brief as either of the following:

Today, in fellowship with the whole family of Christ, we pray for *the churches in India.*
O Lord, in the company of all your people, we call upon your Name for our brothers and sisters in *the churches of India.*

An exhortation of this sort might also introduce the regular series of prayers in the agenda or order of worship, or precede the common recitation of the "Our Father".

Churches accustomed to worshipping in a free style will discover several options for using the suggestions "For Prayer and Intercession". A time might be set aside to hear the pastor or another person describe the churches of the country or region; then the congregation will be led in prayer, using all or part of the suggested biddings and perhaps adding some material of more current or special interest. Another possibility is that the pastor should simply include suggested prayers or biddings in the pastoral prayer (in some traditions called the "general prayer" or "morning prayer") led from the pulpit.

6. Relating the Prayers to Other Parts of the Liturgy and the Life of the Congregation

Prayer for all God's people need not of course be confined to those parts of the worship service formally allotted to intercession, adoration, petition and thanksgiving. We can share with God and each other our concern for, and identification with other members of the Body of Christ at other moments in our worship and at other times in our congregational life.

It is, for example, possible to enlarge the function of announcements and notices so that we share news not only about our own parish or denomination but also about our brothers and sisters in faith who live in other places. And words need not be the only means of conveying information at the time of announcements. A children's church school class might make banners of the eastern and western hemispheres on which to pin the bright-coloured shapes of the countries and regions on the appropriate week. Parish notice-boards, worship bulletins and newsletters can also be used to make information available for regular prayer.

The sermon and the curriculum of religious education in the local church provide other opportunities for enlarging the vision of the congregation and quickening its concern and sense of responsibility for the world-wide community of faith. This book is not intended to provide ready-made sermons, but the passages from the Bible suggested for a given Sunday may well take on new meaning and significance if they are read with the history and task of a particular group of churches in mind.

Making a success of any of these possibilities obviously requires sufficient absorption and augmentation of the background material provided in a given week. And no doubt the simplest way is for the priest or pastor to digest the information and find appropriate methods of sharing it with the congregation. But it could be much more advantageous for a group within the congregation to assume responsibility for carrying out this task. A women's organization, a youth club, a church school class, the worship committee or ecumenical affairs task force might be ready to make the ecumenical cycle of prayer its special project and present the material in a variety of ways and settings.

7. A Special Worship Service

From time to time it might be valuable to create an entire worship event around the theme of sharing and identifying with a particular branch of God's family. In some traditions it is possible for such a service to replace the regular act of worship on Sunday. In other traditions the event would take place at another time. But in either case a worship service entirely devoted to the theme of fellowship with Christians in other parts of the world requires a good deal of preparation on the part of many members of the parish.

The following sketch of what such a service might include is, like previous illustrations in this chapter, focussed upon our relationship with the churches of India (Week 35). It is designed for an Evangelical parish in the inner city of a major metropolitan area in the Federal Republic of Germany (see Week 25). You will need to bear both of these circumstances in mind when considering how you might adapt the ideas to your own situation.

The basic point which the service is intended to emphasize and express is that both communities—the local parish and the churches abroad—each have their own particular burdens to bear and their own special gifts to share.

1. Setting: the service need not be held in the church building and it may well be best to have a place where it is possible to be informal and to make extensive use of visual material.

2. Introduction: as members of the congregation arrive they are greeted by those who have prepared the service, and as they gather they share in a period of silent meditation in order to become used to the different worship environment.

3. Hymn of Praise: this should be a hymn utterly familiar to the congregation—one they can sing almost from memory.

4. Introit: for example, Psalm 47, verses 1, 5-9. This Psalm can be spoken in various ways. It can be read as it is written, with the first verse used as a refrain. Or it can be given interpolations:

> Clap your hands, all you nations—
> French, Indians, Koreans south and north!
> Americans, Russians, people of Madagascar,
> and from all the Indonesian isles!
> Clap your hands, all you nations,
> acclaim our God with shouts of joy. . . .

As this gets going, people might be induced to do what the Psalm suggests—clap their hands. But the introit should end in silence, after which the *Gloria patri* can be recited or sung in a traditional manner.

5. Confession of Sins: this could be in a traditional form or newly written for the occasion and handed out in leaflet form. It might be phrased in fairly general terms or it might involve specific mention of the impact that some aspects of Indian traditions and thought-patterns are having on our society. The text could be spoken by a worship leader alone or shared between a leader and the congregation.

6. Declaration of Forgiveness and Assurance of Grace: this might be in a traditional form or specially composed for the occasion. Emphasis on the solidarity of the human race, under God and in union with Christ, is important.

7. *Collect:* this can be the collect appointed for the day or some other collect—ancient or newly-written—suitable for the occasion.

8. *Bible-Reading(s):* chosen to illuminate the theme of the service and to show the basis of Christian community and concern.

9. *Hymn of Common Concern:* this should express the oneness of the Church and the unity in Christ of all Christian people.

10. *Meditation and Reflection:* this can include other elements besides a sermon or address. Pictures, in the form of slides or posters, might be used. So might music from the region—performed live or recorded. The witness of persons who have visited the country concerned or have a relationship with it in some other way would obviously be helpful. In a large urban area it might be possible to invite citizens of that country who are living nearby to take part in the service.

11. *Affirmation of Faith:* this could be one of the ancient Creeds or some other bold statement of belief. Its position after the Meditation and Reflection is important in order to give it the whole impact of the witness of God's people at all times and in all parts of the world. A brief introduction may be needed to make this point very specifically.

12. *Prayers of Thanksgiving and Intercession:* based on the section "For Prayer" in the ecumenical prayer cycle, together with intercessions for our own country and church, and for the whole Body of Christ. The prayers culminate in the saying of the "Our Father".

13. *Benediction:* a familiar form of blessing might be used, or, when available, a form of blessing from the country concerned.

The service might be followed by the congregation sharing some refreshments, perhaps even a whole meal. It might well take the form of an Agape.

Alphabetical Index of Countries

231

Ecumenical Prayer Cycle in the years 1979-1983

To help ensure that all use the same material each Sunday, we offer here comparative calendars for 1979-1983.

	1979	1980	1981	1982	1983
	beginning Sunday	beginning Sunday	beginning Sunday	beginning Sunday	beginning Sunday
Week 1	Dec. 31, (1978)	Dec. 30, (1979)	Dec. 28, (1980)	Dec. 27, (1981)	Dec. 26, (1982)
Week 2	Jan. 7	Jan. 6	Jan. 4	Jan. 3	Jan. 2
Week 3	Jan. 14	Jan. 13	Jan. 11	Jan. 10	Jan. 9
Week 4	Jan. 21	Jan. 20	Jan. 18	Jan. 17	Jan. 16
Week 5	Jan. 28	Jan. 27	Jan. 25	Jan. 24	Jan. 23
Week 6	Feb. 4	Feb. 3	Feb. 1	Jan. 31	Jan. 30
Week 7	Feb. 11	Feb. 10	Feb. 8	Feb. 7	Feb. 6
Week 8	Feb. 18	Feb. 17	Feb. 15	Feb. 14	Feb. 13
Week 9	Feb. 25	Feb. 24	Feb. 22	Feb. 21	Feb. 20
Week 10	March 4	March 2	March 1	Feb. 28	Feb. 27
Week 11	March 11	March 9	March 8	March 7	March 6
Week 12	March 18	March 16	March 15	March 14	March 13
Week 13	March 25	March 23	March 22	March 21	March 20
Week 14	April 1	March 30	March 29	March 28	March 27
Week 15	April 8	April 6	April 5	April 4	April 3
Week 16	April 15	April 13	April 12	April 11	April 10
Week 17	April 22	April 20	April 19	April 18	April 17
Week 18	April 29	April 27	April 26	April 25	April 24
Week 19	May 6	May 4	May 3	May 2	May 1
Week 20	May 13	May 11	May 10	May 9	May 8
Week 21	May 20	May 18	May 17	May 16	May 15
Week 22	May 27	May 25	May 24	May 23	May 22
Week 23	June 3	June 1	May 31	May 30	May 29
Week 24	June 10	June 8	June 7	June 6	June 5
Week 25	June 17	June 15	June 14	June 13	June 12
Week 26	June 24	June 22	June 21	June 20	June 19

	1979	1980	1981	1982	1983
	beginning Sunday	beginning Sunday	beginning Sunday	beginning Sunday	beginning Sunday
Week 27	July 1	June 29	June 28	June 27	June 26
Week 28	July 8	July 6	July 5	July 4	July 3
Week 29	July 15	July 13	July 12	July 11	July 10
Week 30	July 22	July 20	July 19	July 18	July 17
Week 31	July 29	July 27	July 26	July 25	July 24
Week 32	Aug. 5	Aug. 3	Aug. 2	Aug. 1	July 31
Week 33	Aug. 12	Aug. 10	Aug. 9	Aug. 8	Aug. 7
Week 34	Aug. 19	Aug. 17	Aug. 16	Aug. 15	Aug. 14
Week 35	Aug. 26	Aug. 24	Aug. 23	Aug. 22	Aug. 21
Week 36	Sept. 2	Aug. 31	Aug. 30	Aug. 29	Aug. 28
Week 37	Sept. 9	Sept. 7	Sept. 6	Sept. 5	Sept. 4
Week 38	Sept. 16	Sept. 14	Sept. 13	Sept. 12	Sept. 11
Week 39	Sept. 23	Sept. 21	Sept. 20	Sept. 19	Sept. 18
Week 40	Sept. 30	Sept. 28	Sept. 27	Sept. 26	Sept. 25
Week 41	Oct. 7	Oct. 5	Oct. 4	Oct. 3	Oct. 2
Week 42	Oct. 14	Oct. 12	Oct. 11	Oct. 10	Oct. 9
Week 43	Oct. 21	Oct. 19	Oct. 18	Oct. 17	Oct. 16
Week 44	Oct. 28	Oct. 26	Oct. 25	Oct. 24	Oct. 23
Week 45	Nov. 4	Nov. 2	Nov. 1	Oct. 31	Oct. 30
Week 46	Nov. 11	Nov. 9	Nov. 8	Nov. 7	Nov. 6
Week 47	Nov. 18	Nov. 16	Nov. 15	Nov. 14	Nov. 13
Week 48	Nov. 25	Nov. 23	Nov. 22	Nov. 21	Nov. 20
Week 49	Dec. 2	Nov. 30	Nov. 29	Nov. 28	Nov. 27
Week 50	Dec. 9	Dec. 7	Dec. 6	Dec. 5	Dec. 4
Week 51	Dec. 16	Dec. 14	Dec. 13	Dec. 12	Dec. 11
Week 52	Dec. 23	Dec. 21	Dec. 20	Dec. 19	Dec. 18

Sources and acknowledgements

We wish to thank all those who have granted permission for the use of prayers in this book. We have made every effort to trace and identify correctly all the prayers, and to request all the necessary permissions for reprinting. If we have erred in any way in the acknowledgements, or have unwittingly infringed any copyright, we apologize sincerely, and shall be glad to make the necessary corrections in subsequent editions of this book.

Week 1, from *The Coptic Liturgy*, Coptic Orthodox Patriarchate, Cairo. Week 2, from *Venite Adoremus II*, WSCF, Geneva. Week 3, R. N. Rodenmayer: *The Pastor's Prayer Book*, Oxford University Press, London. Week 4, from the *Liturgy of the Ethiopian Orthodox Church*. Week 5, from Fritz Pawelzik: *I Sing Your Praise All the Day Long*, Friendship Press, New York. Week 6, from Fritz Pawelzik: *I Lie on My Mat and Pray*, Friendship Press, New York. Week 7, from Chinua Achebe: *No Longer at Ease*, William Heinemann Ltd., London. Week 8, from Fritz Pawelzik: *I Sing Your Praise All Day Long*, Friendship Press, New York. Week 9 and 10, as week 8. Week 11, from *A United Liturgy for East Africa*, St. Paul's United Theological College, Limuru. Week 12, from *Venite Adoremus II*, WSCF, Geneva. Week 13, permission from the author. Week 14, from *A Book of Common Prayer*, Gen. Secr. of the Synod of the Church of the Province of South Africa. Week 15, translated and adapted from *La Prière Œcuménique*, Les Presses de Taizé. Week 16, from *Venite Adoremus II*, WSCF, Geneva. Week 17, specially written for this book. Week 18, adapted from *Roman Missal*, Mass for the Unity of the Church, in *La Prière Œcuménique*, Les Presses de Taizé; St. Francis of Assisi also from *La Prière Œcuménique*. Week 19, from *Venite Adoremus II*, WSCF, Geneva; Karl Barth, translated and adapted from *Gebete*, Chr. Kaiser, Munich. Week 20, from *Venite Adoremus II*, WSCF, Geneva. Erasmus, from *A Book of Services and Prayers*, Independent Press Ltd., London; Huub Oosterhuis, from *Your Word is Near*, Paulist Press, New York. Week 22, from *Uniting in Hope*, WCC, Geneva. Week 23, from *The Book of Common Prayer* (1622), Crown copyright in England; William Bright, from *A Book of Services and Prayers*, Independent Press Ltd., London. Week 24, from *Venite Adoremus II*, WSCF, Geneva. Week 25, translated and adapted from Martin Luther's *Betbüchlein* of 1522. Week 27, from a Russian Orthodox Liturgy; Armenian Liturgy, from *La Prière Œcuménique*, Les Presses de Taizé. Week 28, from E. Payne and St. F. Winward: *Orders and Prayers for Church Worship*, The Carey Kingsgate Press, London. Week 29, from the Hong Kong Christian Council. Week 30, from *Venite Adoremus II*, WSCF, Geneva. Week 31, from D. J. Fleming: *The World At One in Prayer*, Harper & Row, New York. Week 32, from Edmond S. P. Jones (ed.): *Worship and Wonder*, Galliard, Great Yarmouth. Week 33, from *Venite Adoremus II*, WSCF, Geneva. Week 34, from *Inauguration Services Church of Pakistan*. Week 35, from *SOEPI 17*, WCC, Geneva. Week 36, from D. J. Fleming: *The World At One in Prayer*, Harper & Row, New York. Week 37, as week 36. Week 38, A. Sitompol and F. Kaan, specially written for this book; F. Ukur, from *The Worship of the 1977 Assembly of the CCA*, Penang. Week 39, from *Week of Prayer for Christian Unity* material, 1978. Week 41, permission from the author. Week 42, Tito de Alencar, from *The World At One in Prayer*, Harper & Row, New York; Dom Hélder Camara, extract from *Prayer for the Rich*, published in Rapidas, the magazine of the Movement for Latin American Evangelical Unity. Week 43, from *Selected Poems* by L. S. Senghor, Oxford University Press, London. Week 44, from *Prayers of the New Man*. Week 45, from Rapidas. Week 46, from *Sing a New Song*, ed. by N. Dexter and P. Jordan, Caribbean Conference of Churches. Week 47, from Ernesto Cardenal: *Zerschneide den Stacheldraht*, Jugenddienst Verlag, Wuppertal. Week 48, from *Venite Adoremus II*, WSCF, Geneva. Week 49, from *A Traveler's Prayer Book*, The Upper Room, Nashville. Week 50, from an ecumenical committee for the Participation of Other Christians in the 41st Eucharistic Congress 1976, Philadelphia. Week 51, from the Centre for Ecumenism in Montreal. Week 52, from *The Roman Missal*, Collins, London.

For your own notes

For your own notes